JAMES LAST

james last

HOWARD ELSON

PROTEUS BOOKS LONDON AND NEW YORK

I would like to express my great thanks to several people whose help in compiling this book was invaluable. To Madeline Bell, Peter Boosey, Anne Holmes, Sue Johnson, David Martin, Barry Reeves . . . and my friend, Roger Whittaker.

And to James Last for the inspiration.

Thank you.

HOWARD ELSON 1982

PROTEUS BOOKS is an imprint of
The Proteus Publishing Group

UNITED STATES
PROTEUS PUBLISHING CO., INC.
9, West 57yh Street, Suite 4504,
New York, NY 10019
distributed by:
THE SCRIBNER BOOK COMPANIES, INC.
597 Fifth Avenue
New York, NY 10017

UNITED KINGDOM
PROTEUS (PUBLISHING) LIMITED
Bremar House,
Sale Place
London W2 1PT

ISBN 0 86276 120 4 (paperback)
ISBN O 86276 174 3 (hardback)

First published in U.S. 1983
First published in U.K. 1982

Design: John Fitzmaurice
Editors: Kay Rowley and Mike Brecher
Typeset: SX Composing Ltd.
Printed by Printer Industria Grafica sa,
Barcelona, Spain
D.L.B. 29284 – 1982

Photo credits:
Photographs courtesy of Deutsche Gramaphon, Barry Plummer, David Redfern, Andre Csillag and Mike Putland/LFI.

CONTENTS

INTRODUCING . . .
JAMES LAST

*i*N THESE DAYS WHEN POPULAR MUSIC TASTES change from moment to moment – heavy metal giving way to reggae; soul giving way to punk; country rock giving way to electronic sounds – James Last has proved himself to be a constant source of beautiful orchestral arrangements and his music has remained outstandingly popular throughout the world for many, many years.

James Last has observed all these musical trends, and noted their development, and absorbed much of the material into his own inimitable style of playing . . . and his arrangements have certainly enhanced them all.

He has also managed to break down the barriers of musical snobbery by not only bringing pop and rock music to the mass easy listening audience, but the classics as well.

Over the last few years, I have been privileged to work with him on many occasions and I have always found him charming, very warm and generous. It is a delight to be in his company. As an artist, he is professional to the core and brilliant.

This book is a personal look at the man himself, through the eyes of the people who know and work for him – his musicians, his singers, his fans.

James Last's track record speaks louder than any words, and what he has achieved in recent years is nothing short of sensational. The man is a genius. And I am pleased to call him my friend.

ROGER WHITTAKER

PORTRAIT OF JAMES LAST

POLYDOR 1236 071

*t*HE ROYAL ALBERT HALL IN London was packed to its ornamental rafters.

They were there in their thousands. Bank managers rubbing shoulders with shopkeepers. Solicitors rubbing shoulders with policemen. Company directors rubbing shoulders with shop stewards. And many, many more besides.

Tonight they had all left their troubles behind them at the door; tonight they were going to enjoy themselves totally, and they knew they wouldn't be disappointed.

Banners waved, streamers and balloons cascaded through the high-domed sky above a brightly coloured sea of people, with even brighter, happy faces. Carnival night had come to the grand old building that Queen Victoria had commissioned to the memory of her beloved German Prince.

Tonight, it was an apt dedication.

The atmosphere inside the mighty Concert Hall was electric. Exciting. Mesmerising – and the air filled with the high-tension of expectancy as the lights dimmed.

The massive crowd was hushed for a moment more as the neatly dressed orchestra struck up the first few notes of their opening number. The night was young.

The musicians managed only to reach the fourth bar of *Fanfare For The Common Man* before the Hall erupted into a frenzy of shouts and cheers, whistles and multitudinous applause, as the bank managers, shopkeepers, solicitors, policemen, company directors, shop stewards, and many, many more besides rose to their feet as one, to greet the very special man to whom they had come to pay homage. By comparison, the last night of the Proms looked like an end of term beano for sixth-formers.

As the fantastic stereo sound emanating from the 60-piece orchestra filled every single nook and cranny of the old Royal building with perfect clarity and precision, a tall, lean, distinguished-looking gentleman emerged from out of the backstage shadows to walk slowly into the piercing beam of the spotlight centre stage to meet his friends. Every deliberate step was greeted with even more tumultuous applause. A crescendo of noise. And in that single moment, ten thousand voices roared their approval in welcome, as twenty thousand hands shot to the sky in salute. It was awe-inspiring.

Hansi was back in town.

It was going to be another long and memorable night, filled with emotion. Queen Victoria would not have been amused . . . she would have been delighted.

Tonight, London belonged to James Last, but the wild and exciting scene of love and happiness and adulation had been played out many times before in Tokyo, Toronto, Sydney, Hong Kong, Singapore, Manila, Dublin, Paris, Rome, Copenhagen, Stockholm, Brussels, Hamburg, and even Moscow, such is the amazing worldwide popularity of a man, who in less than twenty years has become an international superstar in the truest meaning of the word. And a man who has spread happiness around the globe with the ease of spreading butter on his bread, through a very special kind of music.

Someone once wrote: "In London, the Mecca of popular music, he is rated as the most perfect sound machine ever heard. Dutchmen reckon he's worth his weight in gold. Russians think he's worth his weight in vodka, borshtsh and caviar. Indonesians smuggle his records across from Singapore. New Zealanders reckon he's one of their relations. About five per cent of all records in Canada are James Last records. In Germany, this man is celebrated as a prophet in his own country." Yet, they understated their case. James Last is quite simply the most prolific, best-selling recording artist in Europe, an outstanding success story . . . and in short, a modern-day *phenomenon*!

It is hard to keep tracks on Last's continued international success for the simple reason that he is *such* a prolific record maker, producing new albums, that would make a car production line look slow by comparison. At one stage in his career, he was recording fifteen new albums each year at a rate of just under one

LP each month, though today his output is down to a mere twelve a year. And as each new record hits the market, it is eagerly snapped up immediately by his increasing army of fans and followers who dote on every single musical note he makes. Needless to say, his albums carve huge craters in hit parades all over the world . . . and that is *without* taking into account the cassette and cartridge field of operations.

The facts speak for themselves, but even these can't accurately keep pace with his sensational achievements. As soon as one set of statistics on his record sales are published, they are immediately out of date as up pops another new album, another new million-seller, another chart-buster. James Last makes even Midas look redundant.

For the record, however, since 1965, Last has made over 200 albums which in terms of global sales have amassed nearly 60,000,000 copies, rewarding the man with over 160 Gold Discs. The number of Silver Discs that are etched with his name, doesn't bear contemplating.

The figures are, of course, approximate, because as his percussionist Barry Reeves says — "It's impossible to keep tabs on just how many records James Last sells worldwide. I'm sure they've got a man at Polydor to do just that, but I bet even he finds it hard going. I do know, however, that whenever we set out on concert tours, it becomes embarrassing the number of new Gold and Silver Discs that are showered on him. It becomes a regular occurrence in every single country we play. In Holland, say, he'll receive another Gold record for an album which has already gained him five Gold Discs in other territories. In England, he'll pick up another set for a completely different series of records. And it goes on all the time — it becomes monotonous. Wherever we go, you can bet Hansi will receive a handful of Gold and Silver records. It's never ending and I often wonder if even *he* knows how many he has collected."

In 1977, when his album sales had been assessed at topping the 40,000,000 mark worldwide, one reliable source put James Last in fifth place overall as the artist with the biggest album sales, behind The Beatles, who led the field, Mantovani, Herb Alpert and Elton John, but ahead of The Rolling Stones, Frank Sinatra and Elvis Presley. Today, while the album sales of those ahead of him have declined sharply, with the exception of The Beatles, James Last's records have *increased* considerably, and he must surely now have leap-frogged into second place in the worldwide chart. The summit might well be within his grasp in just a handful of years.

Yet, the man whose music has made him the most successful musician in the history of Germany and a multi-millionaire to boot, remains unaffected by his overwhelming world standing, and enormous success. He's almost embarrassed by it all.

Hansi shuns publicity, preferring to spend his time in the bosom of his family, or relaxing in the company of his musicians, away from all the hullabaloo and razz-matazz of showbusiness. And as one journalist wrote:

"His normality is his greatness".

In one interview that hinted at his outstanding wealth, Hansi said: "Money has never meant anything to me. Before I started producing records, when I was with the NDR band arranging in the studio, I would treat the boys to drinks and a meal after the session when I couldn't afford it."

He told another writer: "I'm not a star, because I think when you're a singer you are more of a star. I don't think people should allow themselves to be changed by success. That's wrong. I think it is a kind of success to be accepted as a normal person, not as a star."

Although he doesn't care for the harsh lights and high-powered sparkle of the entertainment world, thinking it false and potentially dangerous, James Last is a man who certainly *does* care a great deal about people. And stories abound about his generosity towards them. Hansi has used his success and great wealth to bring enormous benefits to others.

In 1974, James Last donated the entire proceeds raised by a massive open-air concert in Berlin, amounting to well over £20,000 to the Children's Spastic Society in Berlin and the Campaign to help the famine in war-torn Ethiopia. A year later, in September 1975, he made a lightning visit to London to hand over cheques to the value of £32,000 to officials of Oxfam and Cancer Research — part of the royalties from his best-selling album *James Last Live* — saying that he had decided to donate the money after his conscience had been stirred by appreciative calls from hospitals when he was on his last worldwide tour.

More recently, several albums — including compilation LPs on which he has appeared with a galaxy of other recording artists — have been produced solely for charitable causes, in particular the German Cancer Society and the Father Damien Society for Lepers in Belgium. There are a lot more besides.

And in October 1980, following the tragic death a year before of Joanne Stone, a former member of the James Last Choir, Hansi got together with a few friends, including Cliff Richard, to present a marvellous concert in London to the memory of the young singing star. All the money raised went to her family.

Peter Boosey has been the secretary and guiding light behind the James Last Worldwide Appreciation Society now since he formed it in 1974, knows the man better than most and can reel off similar stories. Even today, he is constantly amazed by Last's tremendous attitude towards other people, particularly his fans.

"He's the most genuine man I have ever met," he says. "He's remarkable and no words I can say can do him enough justice. Yet, it is the little things that make Hansi stand head and shoulders above his contemporaries.

"A couple of years ago in Manchester, James Last was approached at the Stage Door before a concert, by a man who asked him if he could possibly sign an autograph for his mother who was confined to a wheelchair and couldn't come herself. He also told him that she was waiting outside at the front of the theatre.

"Hansi refused.

"Instead, he went with the man, right round to the front of the building, through the milling crowds, and took charge of his mother's wheelchair personally. Then he guided it all the way back to the Stage Door and backstage, where he took the lady round to meet all the members of the Orchestra and the tour staff, before entertaining her to drinks in his dressing room.

"Just before the show was due to start, Hansi picked up the wheelchair and carried it down to the stage and lifted it over the footlights into the auditorium, where the lady was able to take up her position to see the show *without* having to go round to the front of the theatre again. It made her day.

"That's an exceptional story, and I'm sure that many other artists of similar standing have exactly the same feelings as Hansi, but I can't imagine any one of them devoting that amount of time to one fan, least of all taking the trouble he did.

"Another time, Hansi had built up a very good friendship with a young girl and her boyfriend who lived in Sheffield. They were regular concert-goers and Last would often invite them backstage for a drink after a show. They got on very well indeed.

"Several months after their last meeting, however, the girl was tragically killed in a car crash. And when Hansi heard the news, he was shattered and wanted to help. So he invited the girl's boyfriend and her sister to be his special guests at his Hamburg Carnival concerts in January 1982, and paid all their expenses.

"These aren't isolated incidents, there are many, many more such stories. But it's things like these that make James Last so very special to us all. He's the most down-to-earth person I know and totally unaffected by his outstanding success."

Success, however, *has* brought James Last many of the finer things in life, including a large mansion on the outskirts of Hamburg, complete with indoor, heated swimming pool that empties and turns into a dance floor at the press of a button. It's his one concession to stardom.

But one of his proudest possessions is a large leisure complex he designed and built at his own expense, just 100 kilometres from Hamburg, especially for the members of his orchestra. At this superb building in the tiny village of Flintel, the band has everything it needs to relax after working in the studios or out on the road. It was Hansi's way of saying "thank you" to them for all the hard hours they have devoted to him over the years.

The complex was built in 1973 at a cost of nearly £100,000 if you include the land . . . and it is magnificent. Affectionately known as "The James Centre", the building stands in two-and-a-half acres of grounds, containing tennis courts, a miniature soccer pitch, a

swimming pool and crazy golf course. Inside the complex, there are six large and sumptious bedrooms each with its own bathroom, a kitchen, bar, band room, living room and cellar. There is also a special suite of rooms for Hansi's personal use, comprising bedroom, bathroom, kitchen and bar. Dominating the suite, however, is a large piano on which the maestro spends much of his time working out new and fabulous arrangements for forthcoming albums and tours.

It's a well-known fact, that James Last has built up a vast reputation for himself as the ideal employer. The best in the business. As a boss, he is second to none – ask any of the people who work for him – and he rewards his musicians handsomely. Not only are they among the highest paid musicians in the world, they are also the most pampered, courtesy of Hansi. Flintel is only a small part of the story. James Last looks after their every need.

When touring, he books them into the best hotels and the most expensive restaurants, while for travelling to and from each new engagement, he has provided a luxurious, custom-built super-coach, complete with bar and kitchenette. Each year, he gives the musicians *and* their families, at least one all-expenses paid holiday either in his own summer home in Florida, or Spain . . . or for that matter, wherever they want to go.

In 1974, James Last was set to break new ground even for him by undertaking an extensive tour of America. At the last moment, however, the tour was cancelled, and everyone was disappointed but undeterred, Hansi arranged for the entire orchestra to take a three day vacation in Las Vegas – on the house!

When in the company of his musicians, James Last insists on being treated just like one of the boys in the band. He's basically one of them, and loves to be involved in their revelry. He encourages it, too, and often instigates much of the party-going. And it is in these light-hearted moments away from the pressures of performing, that Hansi has built up another huge reputation for himself as the perennial practical joker. He thinks nothing of taking over a hotel bar after a show, and treating everyone there – musicians or no – to drinks

on the house, and he is often found behind the bar, serving them up. Hopefully, someone will partake with him in a glass of his own very special cocktail – the Hansi Special, which comprises two parts vodka, two parts cointreau, topped up with champagne and orange juice to colour. And you believe him when he tells you that it's very potent.

When the drinking starts, it's time for the band to indulge in the grand old pastime of Cardinal Pouff – a favourite party piece.

Peter Boosey again: "A few years ago, my wife and I went with some friends, to see James Last performing in Antwerp.

"After the concert we were all invited to a Flemish restaurant for a meal, where the band was in high spirits even before we had arrived.

"During the course of the evening, I kept hearing incessant banging noises followed by hearty roars of 'Cardinal Pouff' and uproarious laughter, coming from the direction of the musicians. Everyone was having an hilarious time. As the evening progressed, the banging got louder and the laughter stronger.

"So I went over to one of the musicians I knew particularly well and asked him to explain what all the fuss was about. He didn't only tell me . . . he initiated me into the grand order of Cardinal Pouff, which is basically a game which Hansi and the boys play during riotous moments of relaxation.

"Before the game begins, however, a contestant is given a half-pint glass filled with his favourite brew. He then has to execute a series of manoeuvres with great dexterity, but always remembering the correct sequence in which each move is made.

"At the start of the game, the contestant picks up his drink, using only the forefinger and thumb of each hand, and takes a sip. He puts the glass down and shouts 'I drink to the Cardinal *once*'. Next, he must tap on the top of the table with both forefingers, then underneath the table top, and finally – using the same two fingers – touch the tops of his knees, before standing up and sitting down again. The practice is then repeated. 'I drink to the Cardinal *twice*' – only this time, every

manoeuvre is duplicated. Two sips of the drink, two taps and so on.

"Finally, he has to go through the entire procedure for a third time, repeating every single move *three* times in succession. When he has finished the game, he must either drink everything down that is still remaining in his glass, or pour the entire contents over his head. There is, however, a penalty if he makes a mistake on the way and gets the sequence wrong. Then, he must first down the contents of his glass before it is refilled . . . and the game has to be re-started, from the beginning.

"As you can imagine, everybody ends up legless, but it's marvellous fun. One of the English singers introduced the game to the band over ten years ago, and it has since become a national pastime. They have used it to catch unsuspecting guests ever since.

"Hansi tells a story where they played 'Cardinal Pouff' on board an aircraft during a tour of Australia, and several other passengers on board became absolutely paralytic."

Hansi's practical jokes are not, however, confined to moments of relaxation. Sometimes they happen on stage, right in front of the audience, as David Martin – a former member of the James Last Choir – found out with hilarious consequences.

"When you are out on tour with Hansi and the boys, you can imagine that anything goes," he says. "Everyone plays jokes on each other, and the trick is to find out who is the most gullible. After lengthy tours, the joke *has* to be exceptional to catch someone out. You become very wary. But by the end of the schedule . . . chaos reigns.

"During the course of one British tour, Hansi played a superb prank on the members of the choir, which even the audience was allowed to share.

"For the entire series of concerts, the running order for each show was planned to allow the choir to finish its songs on a superb rendition of *Argentina*, with a fantastic arrangement by Hansi. As soon as the number was completed, we would all rise from our seats, move down to the front of the stage, take our bows and then leave the stage – hopefully to thunderous applause. For us, that was the end of our night's work. But not so the orchestra, and they had to run through one final block-busting number as a finale, which usually took up to ten minutes to complete.

"We were the lucky ones in that respect because by coming off stage early, it allowed us the time to nip back to our dressing rooms, change out of our sweat-soaked stage costumes and into more comfortable attire, *and* enjoy the luxury of a few drinks, before it was time to pick up the bus back to the hotel. And this incensed the band, because when they came off stage, dripping wet with perspiration, we would be waiting for them in the wings, hurrying them along and having a right go at them. They had to rush like mad to make the bus on time.

"Each night, the same thing happened . . . until we reached Bournemouth.

"On that particular evening, we ran through our usual routine unaware that anything untoward was in the air. We finished our number, took the bow and hurried off stage for a drink.

"I can remember sitting in the dressing room shortly afterwards, wearing only a pair of underpants, when the tour manager hurried into the room and demanded that we get back on stage, as the audience was shouting for another chorus of *Argentina*.

"Well, you can imagine what we told him to do. But he was adamant and told us to come quickly as Hansi had started to play the introduction to the number. We still thought he was pulling our legs, and that it was all a huge joke, until we actually heard the introduction being played over the tannoy system. Then, panic set in as the boys tried to find some suitable clothes to wear on stage. But unbeknown to us, Hansi and the musicians had hidden all of them . . . except for our trousers.

"Quickly as a flash we struggled into them, as the tour manager and various roadies dragged and pushed us down the stairs and on to the stage and the whole choir, in various stages of undress, including the girls, timidly cowered out in front of the spotlights. We must have looked like a motley collection, dishevelled and hauling up our pants, the boys naked from the waist upwards: the girls hurriedly buttoning up shirts and blouses, and combing their hair. And as we shuffled reluctantly out from the wings, the whole theatre erupted into laughter, while the musicians in the orchestra collapsed in hysterics.

"We soon found out it was a put up job and Hansi had let the audience in on the secret. They loved it, although we were left very red-faced. But it was just James Last's way of getting his own back."

It is now seventeen years since James Last first established himself as a major force in international music circles – and in that time, he has brought pleasure to many millions of people the world over through his records, his live appearances and a simple ambition to make people happy. He has also used the success that has come his way to benefit so many others less fortunate than himself without any thoughts of personal praise and without any desire for gain or human accolades.

Through it all, James Last remains a modest man, yet possessing a carefree, happy-go-lucky attitude to life. He has changed little since he became the undoubted megastar he is today.

In interviews, he repeatedly says that his whole world is his music – and the world is a far better place today for his existence.

Hansi rarely talks about his success, preferring to let his music do the talking for him . . . and it speaks an international language of love and peace and happiness. However, he is proud of what he has achieved, although he readily acknowledges that it is team work.

"I feel very good about what we have done," he says. "But really it has been seventeen years of enjoyment."

. . . And there are several thousand bank managers, shopkeepers, solicitors, policemen, company directors, shopstewards, and many, many more besides, who will heartily echo those sentiments.

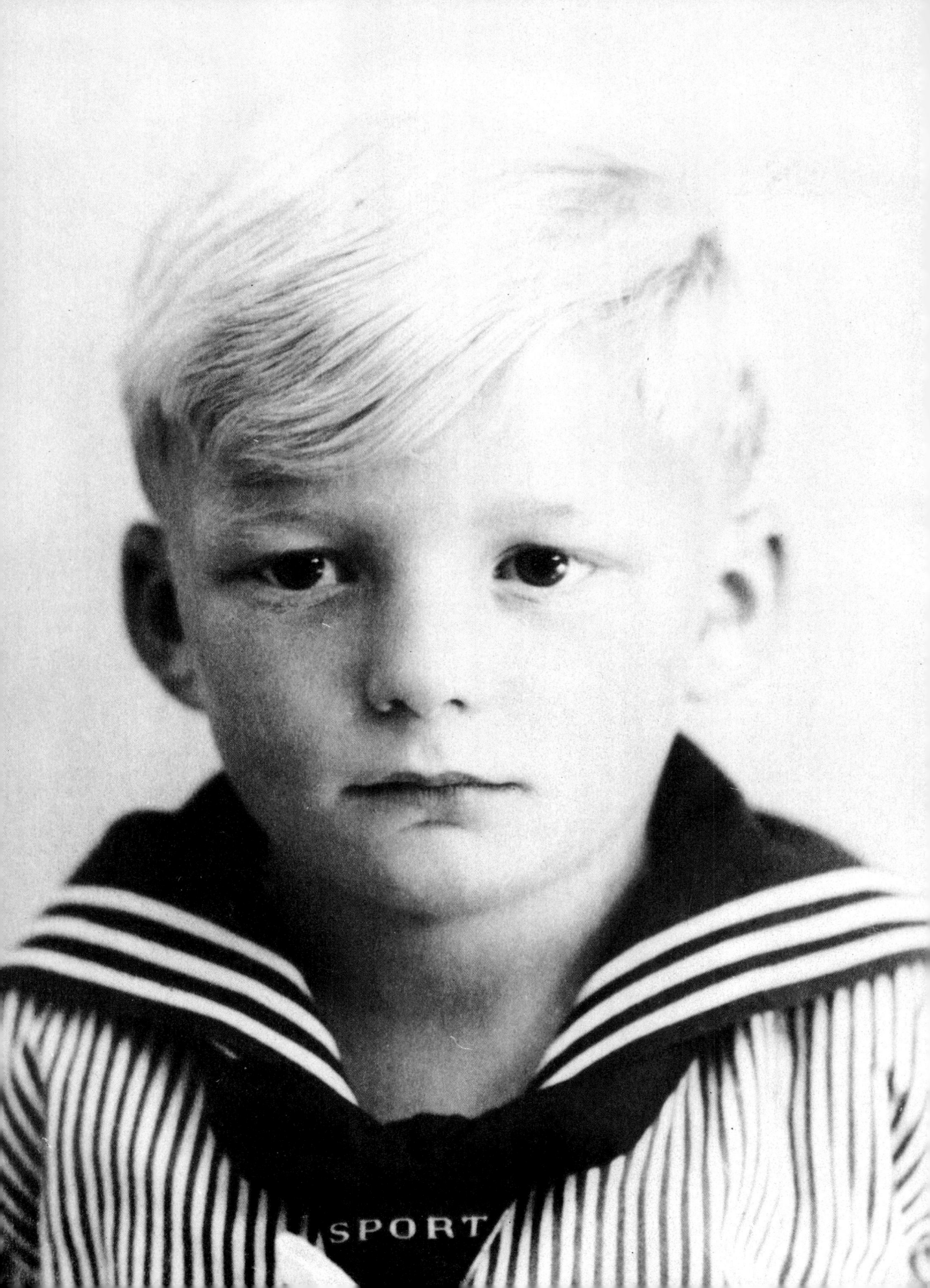

ALBUM TWO

YESTERDAY'S MEMORIES

POLYDOR 2870 117

James Last was born on April 17th, 1929, in the German port of Bremen, the youngest son of local post office worker Louis Last and his attractive wife, Martha. Although he was given the name Hans, right from an early age, the youngster was affectionately known as Hansi.

The Last family wasn't particularly steeped in a long line of musical tradition, although father Louis had a fine ear and a great passion for music of all kinds. He was also more than competent at playing several instruments, including the drums and accordion, yet he took his musical aspirations no further than the amateur stage. He was far too busy building a home and helping to bring up his three sons to possess all the right values in life in a depressed and highly volatile Germany between the wars.

However, nothing gave him greater pleasure than to spend what spare time he had available, making his family happy by playing his own kind of music in the cellar beneath their neat home – and he hoped that one day at least one of his sons might take his lead one stage further and pursue a musical career professionally. Indeed, he gave them every encouragement, though never pushed their development or bombarded them with his own musical ideas. He was simply content to go along with whatever made them happy.

Louis' enthusiasm certainly rubbed off on to his two eldest sons, Robert and Werner, who both inherited their father's interest in music, with Robert – not unnaturally learning to play drums, while Werner took instantly to the accordion. Youngest son, Hansi, however, seemed totally uninterested. His main love at the time was football and he was most upset when at the age of 9, his parents enrolled him for piano lessons with a local tutor. He didn't mind learning to play the piano, it was just that it interfered with his soccer playing and other developing sporting activities.

Still, he gritted his teeth and persevered with the task in hand, though by the age of 10, he was the despair of his music teacher, and his apparent lack of progress led his tutor to make rash criticisms about his ability, or the lack of it. The teacher reported back to Hansi's parents that their son was "totally, completely, undoubtedly *unmusical* – he has not a note of musical ability in his body."

But, within a few years, Hans Last had proved his tutor wrong when at the age of fourteen, he was accepted for a place in the Bremen Music Academy – and later trained at the Army Music School in Frankfurt.

However, by this time, Germany was in the savage grip of war with many inevitable changes on the horizon . . . and at times it seemed that the happy-go-lucky music would never again emanate from the Last family cellar. The family was changing, too. Eldest son, Robert, had been called up for military service and he was destined to be captured by the allies and see out the hostilities as a Prisoner of War. Werner, too, was drafted when his time came and he was eligible to serve his country, leaving only Hans behind to continue with his studies, which by now were thriving.

The youngster fared well, becoming proficient at playing the flute and bassoon, as well as the piano. He had also started to learn double-bass, an instrument on which he showed masterly control and tremendous flair. He seemed to have a natural talent and made spectacular progress, even when his studies were temporarily interrupted by allied bombers who did their best to raze the school to the ground. Hans was forced, along with his fellow students, to move to Bückeburg, near Hannover.

Academic life proved a very strict and regimental existence for the teenager who was far more interested in enjoying himself and having a good time. Still, he never bucked the system and contented himself with being a hard-working scholar, always eager to learn new things and devise new techniques. It was a quality that was to hold him in tremendous stead in later years.

At about the same time, Hans Last developed a love for jazz and dance band music, and he listened to it as often as he could. He also spent much of his spare time improvising jazz arrangements on double bass, hoping that one day he would be able to put this remarkable talent for improvisation into practical use professionally.

He had just turned sixteen when the war in Europe came to a dramatic end; he decided to quit the Music Academy, and returned home to his family in Bremen without really knowing what he was going to do. "If I had continued my musical studies I would probably have become a conductor of serious music by the time I was twenty-four," he now says.

Like much of Germany, Bremen had changed drastically. Allied bombing raids had left much of the city decimated. Chaos and confusion reigned. Although the city was now occupied by the American Forces, almost everything was in short supply, particularly food, money and employment.

However, the Allies brought with them something that was to have a lasting and dramatic effect on the sixteen-year-old boy – music. Beat music, swing, Big Band sounds, boogie-woogie . . . and he found great enjoyment, amid all the misery and depression of a war shattered society, by indulging himself in this 'new' music.

"I used to listen to British and American records on Forces Radio," he says. "The music became a great influence on me."

He also befriended several US servicemen and it wasn't long before they discovered Hansi's amazing talents for making music. So much so, that he was asked to play piano at one of the many servicemen's clubs that had sprung up in Bremen. It was his first professional engagement, although he wasn't paid in hard currency, but packs of American cigarettes, which – being a non-smoker – he sold on the black market to buy food for the family.

Hans Last soon became a regular attraction on Bremen's night club circuit, playing in a band run by Hans-Günter Oesterreich. They played arrangements of the American and British music they had heard on Forces Radio, with a German flavour and approach, and soon became very much in demand for appearances in the US service clubs throughout the area. The band possessed a style of their own, albeit adapted from the cream of the 'foreign' bands they had been listening to, like Benny Goodman, Glen Miller, Ted Heath, Tommy Dorsey and Harry James. The sound was enhanced shortly afterwards by the recruitment of a new drummer – a former Prisoner of War, just back from internment. It was Robert Last – Hansi's brother.

In 1946, Hans-Günter Oesterreich joined Radio Bremen and one of the first things he did on his appointment was to form a Dance Orchestra with which to broadcast to listeners throughout the city. He recruited musicians from his former nightclub band, including Karl-Heinz Becker – who was later to play a major part in the James Last story. He also offered Hans and Robert Last permanent positions. Their brother, Werner – now back in circulation and working in Bremen – also auditioned for a spot, and was accepted immediately. Louis Last's ambition of seeing at least one of his sons as a professional musician had become reality . . . three times over. He was delighted and often joined the boys for impromptu jam sessions in the family cellar when time allowed. He played with them, too, when the family held open house and threw riotous parties for their friends when times were hard and they wanted to forget their troubles for a few hours at least.

"We liked to make good party music," said James Last. "To have fun and get plenty of atmosphere. We liked to have good parties in Germany."

Even then an idea was taking root in Hansi's mind that wouldn't see fruition for nearly twenty years.

The Last Brothers stayed with the Radio Bremen Dance Orchestra which Hansi admits "was also American influenced", for two years during which time they undertook several live engagements besides their studio work. Then in 1948, with their old friend from the night club circuit days – Karl-Heinz Becker – in tow, they left the orchestra and formed the Last-Becker Ensemble . . . and hit the road again, going the rounds of the city's servicemen's clubs once more.

Playing a style of American-based jazz – "I enjoyed the style of Woody Herman very much at that time," says Hansi – the Last-Becker Ensemble flourished. Business was good, engagements flooded in – and the six-piece group was also gaining the attention of the German media, too, with the result that in 1950 Hans Last was voted Top Bassist in a German jazz poll. It was an award he was to win for three consecutive years.

The same year, he met Waltraud Wiese at a party for which the group provided the music. Five years later Waltraud became Mrs. Hans Last. Their daughter Caterina was born in 1958, and son Ronald appeared the following year.

Although the Last-Becker Ensemble was thriving, Hans Last in particular, was becoming restless. He

longed to form his own orchestra and play his own kind of music – and with this in mind, in 1955 he disbanded the group with the main intention of branching out with his own big band. However, he had plenty of ideas, but not too much finance and the Hans Last Orchestra at least for the time being, had to be shelved. So Hansi, now with a wife to support, took a job with the North German Radio Dance Orchestra (the NDR). Within a year, he was writing their arrangements.

His reputation as an arranger started to bubble, and before long, he was called upon to arrange for some of Europe's finest artists including Helmut Zacharias, Freddy Quinn, Caterina Valente . . . and many more. People who knew and worked with him in those days, firmly admit that through these arrangements, the basis of what was later to become known as The James Last Sound, was emerging. And as he progressed, learning new things and developing new ideas, his work as an arranger was very much in demand, particularly from record companies who liked his refreshing new approach to music. One such company was the Deutsche Grammophon/Polydor Company, who were later to sign him to an exclusive contract.

History has it that Last joined Polydor almost on a whim.

For several years, through his arrangements for many of their top recording artists, Polydor had been well aware of the young musician's potential, but as yet they hadn't approached him and offered a permanent position with the company. That, however, wasn't far away.

He told Bob Willox: "One day, when I was working with the NDR I was coming out of work and I said my usual goodnight to the doorman, and I thought, 'You will say goodnight to this man every day for the next thirty years unless you do something about it'. So I went straight to Deutsche Grammophon and asked if I could cut a disc. They said, 'Go ahead'. So I did."

Hansi left the North German Radio Dance Orchestra in 1964. He started to recruit musicians for his own orchestra, using several members of the NDR and his brother Robert . . . and signed a contract with Polydor Records.

Thus began one of the most successful partnerships in the history of popular music. A partnership that flourished almost from the start . . . and continues to thrive with outstanding success today.

Yet, it was to be a whole year before Last would develop his brilliant 'Non-Stop Dancing' formula, that became one of his instantly recognisable trademarks.

His first album *Die Gabs Nur Einmal*, however, didn't exactly set the world on fire. It fizzled slowly. It was a disappointment to Hansi and wasn't sufficiently different enough to herald any kind of musical revolution. But it was a mere spark before a raging conflagration that was about to fire the imagination of the whole record-buying world . . . and Hans Last was shortly to meet up with James Last.

NON-STOP DANCING

POLYDOR 237 447

*a*LL THE TIME HANS LAST HAD BEEN WORKING FOR the North German Dance Orchestra, he had been developing a style, a sound that he hoped to unleash one day, first on the unsuspecting German public – and then, who knows? His mind was alive with ideas, bursting to break out. Though he hadn't quite worked out the right formula.

Last loved parties. Back home in Bremen during those pathetic, poverty-strewn months that followed the end of World War II, the Last family had entertained themselves and their friends and neighbours by throwing parties to keep the spirits high and to boost their sagging morale. The bigger the party, the better – and everybody had a good time. It had become an infectious habit ever since and any excuse for a good old fashioned knees up would do.

Yet for many years now, Hansi had realised that there was something *missing*. The parties just weren't as good as they used to be and he was determined to find out why.

He found the answer almost immediately in the records that were being played. Sure the music was good, but was it the right kind? It seemed just a little dated. And the presentation on record left a lot to be desired. When each number finished, there was a long, almost agonising pause, just when you were letting your hair down and having fun, until the next track played on the album. As often as not, the atmosphere that only minutes before had seemed so vibrant, so exciting and alive, was completely deflated in those seconds of silence. He also determined to do something about *that* if he could.

His idea was simple, and when he joined Polydor, he had the opportunity to put it into practice.

"We liked to have good parties in Germany," he said. "People wanted good music for them, so I set about to provide it. It was as simple as that. I told a guy at Polydor about this and added that most of the time it was not the right music. There was only Ray Conniff and Trini Lopez, and they were playing old music and old titles.

"I said I'd like to do a kind of party music with new songs because at that time there were no instrumental orchestrations of The Beatles' music. There was nothing on the market. No band in the world was playing new songs – just music from the 30's and 40's, without fun, without atmosphere. I wanted to create atmosphere.

"I also realised that there was a big gap in the record market. No big bands were playing the hits of the day and at that time there was a lot of hostility between the generations. Older people wouldn't accept The Beatles' or The Rolling Stones' music because they didn't like the long-haired young people who were playing it. They didn't like the pop voices, crying and screaming the words.

"So I set out to present *their* music in a form that would be acceptable to a much wider audience. We started with songs from The Beatles and Rolling Stones and so on, to make it an easy style to just get the atmosphere. We didn't have any other ambition than to make someone's party more enjoyable."

Although it was a simple technique – taking popular chart material of the day, mixed together with a devastating arrangement, foot-tapping rhythms, a punchy brass section and plenty of atmosphere (which Last describes as "a fun loving sound"), it was highly effective and totally unique in the days when Beatlemania was at its peak and big bands had been dead and buried years before, overtaken by the emergence of rock 'n' roll, a musical development Last had avidly noted.

"I wanted to sound like we were all having fun making it," he says, "because that feeling transmits itself to the listener and makes everyone happy. Good party music, that's all – simple."

But that was easier said than done. Many people had tried before . . . and failed.

He found the key to this simplicity by returning to his musical roots, and listening to Mozart.

"I saw how beautifully simple his approach was and I was much impressed," he adds. "And I tried to apply the lesson. I finally arrived at a formula which was rich, but effortless. I aimed at simplicity working through emotion and feeling, rather than technical achievement."

It worked, too.

In 1965, Last put forward his proposals to a director of the Deutsche Grammophon/Polydor Company, Heinz T. Voigt, who shared his enthusiasm for the project, and decided to give it a try. Shortly afterwards, Polydor issued the resulting album called simply *Non-Stop Dancing '65*, which was recorded entirely in the rapidly emerging – though still in its embryonic days – stereo sound. It proved a masterpiece of achievement, containing every thing Last had set out to do. The album comprised an unheard of twenty-eight numbers, featuring such chart-busting songs as The Beatles' *She Loves You*, *I Want To Hold Your Hand*, and *I Feel Fine*, together with versions of Roy Orbison songs, Chuck Berry, Manfred Mann and Larry Williams, packed tightly together with loads of fun. It was indeed good party music, as Last had insisted it would be, *and* non-stop dancing as the title suggested. Where it was necessary to include a pause due to tracking, the silence was broken with all the cheery sounds of applause, shouting and cheering, just like a real party. Hand-clapping. Revelry. Atmosphere. Last was practising what he preached, and how!

That first album proved a revelation in musical circles and established Last's career in no uncertain terms, almost overnight. It also introduced a new name to the German populus, that of *James* Last. His name was changed by a well-meaning, yet strictly anonymous, Polydor executive, who figured the name Hans lacked commercial possibilities and that James sounded far more international, though as Last admitted, he never intended to produce an *international* 'sound'. "It was

just a happy coincidence and stayed that way."

Non-Stop Dancing '65 became a massive smash hit, not only in Germany, but throughout Europe . . . and much further afield, too. It's instant success surprised a few people, not least of all Polydor Records and Hansi himself. The record broke down the barriers of nationality to appeal to a wide-ranging audience far beyond the German borders, and for once James Last had underestimated his own musical effect. "I never thought of appealing to people outside Germany," he admitted. "As it happened I did, but it was coincidental that I made an international name."

Yet in an almost calculated way, he hit the jackpot in one take.

"Before you start work on an album, you must be sure of your idea from beginning to end, so that you know exactly what you are doing. If you tackle it half prepared, it's no use at all. I had an idea and worked hard on that idea," he says. "It was an attempt to change the form of instrumental music at that time. I wanted to take hit numbers of that time and play them my way. In my style. But I didn't want the sound to be too specialised. The style shouldn't be too difficult for the audience. There are so many bands playing in the world with no style.

"I am a happy man and I like to make happy music. I express myself in my own style."

And happiness certainly seemed to be one of the keys to the secret of James Last's success with the first 'Non-Stop Dancing' album. It had an instant and lasting appeal. Although the music he played was simply a

re-working of old pop tunes, the Last approach to it was breathtakingly new and refreshing. The arrangements masterful. For the first time in many years, he had calmed the troubled waters between the various musical generations. Now, people often described as 'the silent majority' and ranging in age from mid-twenties upwards, were listening to the out-and-out pop music they had once decried as "tuneless rubbish", composed by such members of the long-haired brigade as Paul McCartney and John Lennon, and such blatant rock 'n' rollers as Chuck Berry. This time, however, it was served up courtesy of a man with a unique vision and a sound to match – James Last. It was exactly what they wanted . . . and it sowed the seeds of even greater things to come.

The hardest thing for any artist to do, who has recently established himself on the international music scene with his first hit record, is to follow it up. For many, the dilemma poses unbearable pressures they can't quite come to terms with, and they fail miserably.

For James Last the problem wasn't even considered. He hadn't expected to be instantly successful, it was a bonus and he would just carry on as before. He had created what he believed was a winning formula and he had no reason to doubt its long-lasting potential. After all, he had a wealth of musical compositions to choose from as the international hit parades were changing with every week that passed. As an avid football fan, he realised, too, that you never change a winning team. So, Hansi simply got on with the job of making his happy music. *Non-Stop Dancing '65* gave way to *Non-Stop Dancing '66*, through the 60's and 70's, and into the 80's via numerous *Best Of Non-Stop Dancing* volumes. Each one making prairie fires look slow by comparison with the way they were bought up by record-buyers the world over. What started as a simple idea, turned to Gold, time after time after time. To borrow the title of one recent Last album, Hansimania was rife.

James Last had arrived with a vengeance. His stay was destined to be a long and happy one. He was 34.

JAMES LAST DOES HIS THING

POLYDOR 2418 070

JAMES LAST HAS OFTEN BEEN QUOTED AS SAYING "I don't like people who divide music into categories, because you can't distinguish between classical music and popular music, but only between good music and bad music."

In 1966 he well and truly proved that point when he turned his attention to the classics for inspiration, remembering his days as a young student when he spent many hours attempting to master the musical masterpieces of Beethoven, Schuman, Haydn, Grieg, Bach and, one of his own particular favourites, Mozart. Taking the more popular classics as a starting point, Hansi gave them the James Last treatment and he re-arranged them in his own inimitable style, keeping the simplicity of the originals, yet with a softer approach . . . and plenty of feeling. It worked like a charm and a whole new market place fell under his hypnotic spell.

Through his *Classics* album which sold a million copies in four weeks in Germany alone, and the subsequent *Classics Up To Date* series, the great long-haired, bewigged maestros from the past were now vying for chart positions alongside their modern-day contemporaries. James Last has brought the two together.

After that, it seemed that everything James Last touched, or re-arranged musically speaking, turned into Gold, as he focussed his attention on the entire musical spectrum for creativity. He turned his hand to marches (*Happy Marching*); songs from the sea (*Captain James At Seven Seas*); folk tunes (*Last Of Old England*); operetta (*Happy Lehar*); polkas (*Polka Party*); Country And Western (*Country And Square Dance Party*); Latin American (*In South America*) . . . With so many varying, so many different styles, Hansi had a whole world of music to choose from, to refurbish into that distinctive James Last sound.

"I can never really define 'The James Last Sound'," he has said on many occasions when asked to analyse his music. "It has no real skill."

By 1968, the James Last sound – skillful or no – was the rage of Europe. Album followed album to the top of the charts and his orchestra was voted Top Orchestra Of The Year by the German Record Distributors Organisation. It was just one of many awards from his peers in the music industry that have come his way ever since, *without* taking into consideration any of the Platinum, Gold and Silver Discs that arrive on his doorstep with remarkable regularity. It seems strange, however, that it was only as recently as January 1982 that James Last received Britain's Carl Alan Award as The Most Popular Band. The awards are made annually by the British Dancing Industries for outstanding services to the world of dance. For a man who has given so much to that particular industry over the years, the accolade was long overdue.

There was another side to the success story, too, which also started during the 1960s. Hansi diversified his talents to take in writing and composing. Before long, he had emerged as a song-writer of distinction, penning several hit songs, including *Happy Heart* for Andy Williams, *Games Lovers Play* for Eddie Fisher, *Blame It On Me* for Ray Charles, *Fool* for Elvis Presley, for which he received the American ASCAP Award in 1973, the same year he picked up the Country Music Award from ASCAP, (Nashville, Tennessee), for his song *When The Snow Is On The Rose*.

Yet, a major turning point in his already illustrious and record-breaking career, came in 1969 when he was persuaded to take his orchestra out of the recording studio and on to the road. The public demanded it . . . and always eager to please, such is the make up of the man, Hansi agreed, although he was very apprehensive about the prospects of playing live. But he insisted that when the band went out on tour, it must produce precisely the same sound it created on record – no matter what the expense. He gathered together the very best equipment that was available, and meticulously planned everything down to the most minute detail. Hansi knew he was gambling for high stakes and he wanted to make sure that the odds at least were in his favour.

He also took with him Peter Klemt, his engineer from the Deutsche Grammophon Studios, to ensure that the James Last sound played live, was perfect. Peter guaranteed that it was.

Hansi said later: "I concentrate on a stereo sound. So many bands today make shrill noises that deafen one

part of the audience, yet can't be heard by others. To eliminate the din, I engage a special engineer. He sits by the stage with an instrument that ensures a complete all round stereo effect. People have written to me to say that on record my special sound effects fill the house with a wonderful atmosphere they have never experienced before." James Last, with the help of Peter Klemt, recreated that experience live on stage. It was a marvellous breakthrough.

That first tour, which was confined only to Germany, proved an outstanding artistic triumph for Last and the orchestra, due to his impeccable preparation, but then everyone knew it would be. And like his first 'Non-Stop Dancing' album, it paved the way for things to come. Hansi had at last broken the ice. Now he was preparing to dive in head first.

The tour, however, *didn't* make money and overall Hansi estimated it cost him nearly £250,000 to stage. Subsequent tours, through enormous overheads, have cost him even more as he strives for perfection. "But it is worth it," he says. "I like to give something back to the people who buy my albums. It is also a lot of fun to go out and play live. Everybody enjoys our concerts, the musicians as well as the audience.

"Now I need the reaction of my audience – they

recharge my international batteries. Impressions like this give me new musical ideas which come to life in new productions and compositions."

If the 1969 tour had one memorable highlight amid so many highlights, it came when the orchestra played in Bremen. There were two very special people in the audience that night, Louis and Martha Last – Hansi's parents.

The same year, the James Last Orchestra made their North American debut at the Canadian Expo '69 celebrations, and created the same kind of rapturous reaction it had in Germany a few months earlier.

The Canadian success encouraged Hansi to broaden his horizons even further, starting the same year with a tour of Holland and followed a year later by further domestic engagements, including an appearance at the Berlin Film Festival when the orchestra played at the Grand Ball . . . and a tour of Denmark.

1971 saw the start of what has become a very special and highly personal, (and needless to say successful), association with Britain.

Yet, once again, Hansi admitted to being almost petrified about performing in Britain for the first time. As he said at the time: "I am nervous about my first appearance in England because I have heard they can be

very critical over there. What goes down in Germany might not be right for England. It will mean a week of sleepless nights beforehand.''

He needn't have worried. The tour proved a sell-out with standing-room-only notices displayed outside every theatre he visited. It has been like that ever since.

The James Last conquest of the world was as rapid as it was spectacular. While his records continued to sell in millions, Hansi consolidated all that success by appearing live whenever his recording commitments and studio work allowed. During the early 70's, he broke new ground by visiting South Africa, Australia and New Zealand, the Far East, Hong Kong and Japan. He even took his ''happy music'' behind the Iron Curtain to play an unforgettable series of concerts in the Soviet Union, where 'Non-Stop Dancing' melted even the coldest heart!

Back in Germany in 1972, he celebrated his home-coming, by throwing a massive 'voodoo' party in the Ernst-Merck Halle in Hamburg which was attended by 10,000 happy-go-lucky fans paying homage to the man they had dubbed 'The Prophet' and 'The Party King'. Indeed, the party proved so successful that it has become an annual 2-day event and attracts many thousands of fans from all over the world, whose one intention is let themselves go, to have fun and enjoy themselves . . . and dance to the non-stop party music of James Last.

Since 1965, James Last has continued to do what he does so magnificently well: to make happy music – ''my only ambition is to make people happy. My music

is simple and easy to listen to and people find it relaxing. That's what they want when they come home from a hard day at the office''. Through his hit records and sell-out tours, he has been true to his one aim in life. And he has achieved his goal through sheer hard work and plenty of it. His pace and work-rate at times is phenomenal.

"I work hard,'' he says. "Twenty-four hours a day in the studio when we are recording. At the end, I feel tired, sure, but wow – bubbling inside.''

But all the hard work has paid off in terms of artistic and financial reward, and he admits to being a multi-millionaire, though Hansi is the prime candidate for the title of the 'Happiest Millionaire'.

"It is true that I am a millionaire,'' he says. "But I don't really care about all the money. I just like to make people happy with the sound of my music.

"I lead a normal life. When I started in the music business I was the same as I am now. I was just an arranger and conductor. When the time's over for big success, I can do arrangements. I can write classical music. But it is only hard work that has got me where I am today.

"When I am not working, I like to live life to the full. I live lustily to stop myself getting bored. I don't like getting bored – that is part of the reason I am successful.

"And after a hard day's work, I like to throw big parties. I love parties.''

Which is really how it all started . . .

MUSIC IS MY LIFE

POLYDOR 2437 379

JAMES LAST WAS ONCE DE-scribed by one eminent British national newspaper as "the best boss in the world". He certainly lives up to this name and it is no closely guarded secret that he treats all the musicians who play for him very well indeed, as if they are part of one big happy family. It's an infectious attitude, too.

"I like happy music, so I keep my band happy," he says. "I've been a musician in a band and it is a very hard life. So I try to make life not so hard for *my* musicians. They work hard and they deserve the best.

"We are just one happy family and it shows in the music we play. You can see it on stage. Quite honestly, I have the best band in the world. There is no question about it. They don't have to ask for more money if they work over the times, because they know when they work for Hansi, everything is okay."

Everything certainly *is* okay, judging by the atmosphere and cameraderie within the ranks. And Last's reputation in musical circles has guaranteed that there are dozens of musicians queuing up for the privilege – and the enormous pleasure – of working with him.

Hansi knows the true value of working with musicians of the finest calibre and he respects them all. He never takes them for granted and often collaborates with them on recording sessions and involves them totally on tour. He likes familiarity and is always reluctant to change his musicians . . . "if I can help it." It pays the right dividends, too.

"As an arranger, you have to see the good things in a musician and then make the right arrangements," he says. "So it's on me to find the good guys. That's what we need, good people and it is on me as the father of the group to bring them to the right place. I take all the capabilities of my musicians into account when arranging. To write for them and produce the best in them, I must know them well.

"They know I'm the boss, but I don't like to play the big boss man all the time. I think it's bad to have too great a gap in authority between musicians and bandleader. So if you treat your musicians the right way, they will respect you and play for you.

"We like to have fun together – we work hard together – but it doesn't stop us relaxing together. Touring with the orchestra is fine, but even on tour I like to relax. So that's why I surround myself with happy-go-lucky musicians. As I said, we're one big happy family."

Singer Madeline Bell has been part of the family now since 1979 and in that time she has toured Britain, the Far East, and Europe as a member of the James Last Choir, and worked with Hansi on several recording sessions. She's become an ardent fan.

"During the time I've been with James Last," she says, "it's been great. James Last is all right with me.

"Still, you must realise that it is not a full-time job. No nine to five stuff. I suppose in one year alone, as far as I'm concerned, I must work ten to twelve weeks with the orchestra, on tour, in the recording studio, or on television engagements. And I've no complaints. My association with the man has been marvellous. I'm not saying that everything is sweetness and light, though, because you're bound to get a few problems. You'll always get the odd hassle working with any band, and I've worked with several over the years. But with an orchestra like this, which is just like a circus of sixty people travelling, sleeping and breathing together when you are out on the road, it's only natural there will be a little friction.

"However, Hansi treats everyone magnificently well and I've been treated far better in this band than any other I've toured with. You're not spoilt, but then you're not neglected, either. Everybody knows what they are supposed to do. You do your job well and once the tour starts they take over your brain for the time you are out on the road. They tell you exactly where you are supposed to be, when you're supposed to be there . . . and everything is taken care of, so you know exactly what you have to do. The organisation is terrific and that's just part of James Last's make up. He plans everything meticulously and always strives for perfection.''

Over the years with the continued success of the James Last Orchestra, there have been suggestions from many quarters, that Hansi is an aloof character, almost reserved . . . and he doesn't make friends easily. Madeline Bell refutes the allegations.

''I wouldn't say Hansi was aloof. Far from it, because Number One on my list of points in his favour, is that he travels *everywhere* with the band by bus, if we travel by bus which is usually the case. And it doesn't matter what time we have to leave for our next destination, be it two o'clock in the afternoon or four in the morning, Hansi is always on the bus on time – and he expects everyone else to be there as well.

''If we travel by air, there is no special treatment for the boss man, either. No big deal. No First Class – he travels Tourist Class like everyone else, and that's what I admire about him. He doesn't possess the attitude of 'I'm the big star, I'm going to do the big star bit', which as you probably know, doesn't happen very often with many of his contemporaries.

''As long as I've known him, James Last has never acted like the superstar he undoubtedly is. He's made a lot of money and would have every right to play the prima donna once in a while, but he doesn't. He's not flash. Sure he lives well, and dresses well, and carries himself well, but so he should. Yet, he really is a rarity in this business, suddenly cracking the markets in so many different countries and being one up on so many others. But the big time syndrome is not in his nature. He cares about his music and the people around him, and likes to be involved with them.

''Hansi always has a very personal and close relationship with the band – he's the father of the family, and he's always there if you need him. If the bus breaks down when we're on the road, you'll find him working away with everybody else trying to fix the problem. He certainly doesn't sit back and let everyone else get on with it.''

Madeline also believes Hansi is a super boss to work for.

''At the risk of repeating myself,'' she says, ''James Last *really* is a joy to work for.

''He always says that music is his life and I really do believe that he believes that. It's no publicity stunt. And that's not a bad thing at all, because if *you* believe then everybody believes and this attitude permeates throughout the orchestra. It's fun and everyone involved wants to play for him.

''When you go out on stage, you go out with the attitude of always giving your best and enjoying yourself; of having a good time. If we get down to the dollars and cents of the matter, that's what you are getting paid for. Yet, even if you were doing the gig for nothing, you would still go out there with the same attitude of mind. You can't help it. That's what James Last is all about. His image is that of a happy man – and everybody enjoys themselves. It's the right image, too.

No matter what arguments you might have had with one of the other musicians, no matter what hassles are going on backstage, once you get out in front of the lights, the personality and character of that man gets through to you and wow! You forget your problems instantly and get caught up in the terrific atmosphere of love and happiness. And it extends right over to the other side of the footlights, too. The audience certainly has a great time.''

Madeline Bell was born in Newark, New Jersey, USA, and grew up in an area of extreme poverty. Much of her early life was spent in church and at Sunday school, and it was here that she first experienced music.

''I loved singing and it came naturally to me. I was in every single choir that was going. Singing became a way of life,'' she adds. ''It became a very vital part of my life.

''At school, I joined the glee clubs. I can remember one that was called Four Jacks And A Jill (I was Jill). We sang in school, on street corners – in fact anywhere there was an audience. We entertained in school talent shows and sang in local clubs. However, we never had a backing group, we just sang. It was the only way we knew how.''

At sixteen, she joined her first Gospel Group – The Glovertones–and toured with them all over the Southern States of America. But her singing career really started to take off when she was signed to appear with the Alex Bradford Singers, who were at that time, the most popular Gospel group in America. And for the next few years, she toured extensively all over the USA.

Madeline was also part of the group that appeared off-Broadway in the celebrated 'Black Nativity' production, written around their music by Langston Hughes. It was with the same group that she later came to Britain in the early 1960's and after appearing in 'Black Nativity' on the West End stage, she decided to make London her home, and determined to pursue a solo singing career. In 1964, she made her solo debut at a cabaret club in Newcastle-upon-Tyne.

Shortly afterwards, she was introduced to Dusty Springfield who offered her a job singing sessions – ''and things just snowballed from there,'' she says.

By 1969, she was established as one of the finest session singers in Britain and in great demand for work. That same year, though, she was asked to join a new band – Blue Mink – and for the next five years enjoyed outstanding success with them in the international charts. Maddy sang lead vocals on all Blue Mink's major successes including *Melting Pot*, *Banner Man*, *Stay With Me*, *By The Devil*, *Randy* and *Good Morning Freedom*, and she also toured Britain, Australia, New Zealand and America with the band.

However, during her stint with Mink, Madeline continued with her session work and in 1972 she was asked to record with James Last for the first time. ''I actually went over to Germany to sing on a 'Beach Party' album,'' she says. She had met the man initially two years earlier at a Song Festival in Rio De Janeiro where she became great friends with his wife, Waltraud. The friendship continues today.

"She is one of the finest women I have ever met," admits Madeline. "She is such a lady, such a beautiful person. She is so down to earth and very, very nice. Even though I had nothing to do with the James Last Orchestra at that time, we became great friends. Whenever we met, we greeted each other like long lost, bosom buddies, though in many ways, she is a very reserved lady . . . and her husband is very similar. He is a very shy person and not at all aggressive. He tends to stand back and if you don't know him, you might think he was a little stand-offish, when in actual fact it is not the case at all. Once you have been introduced, and you get to know the man, you realise just what a fantastic person he is. I think the shyness is all down to nerves, he *has* to know someone before he opens up."

When Blue Mink parted company in 1975, La Bell returned to her session singing combining her time with a solo career of her own. Since then, she has become well respected as one of the finest female singers in the business with major appearances in concert and cabaret venues all over the world to her credit. She became a permanent member of the James Last Choir in 1979 as a replacement for her cousin Joanne Stone, and she has enjoyed every minute of the experience.

"The first 'live' gig I ever did for James Last illustrated one of his great qualities," she adds. "And it proved to me that he doesn't like to be over-rehearsed.

"That first engagement was in Japan and I had flown in specially for the show without a single clue as to what was expected from me. I even went on stage not knowing what on earth I was supposed to do. All I had been given was a running order for the programme, nothing more. But I had no idea how each song had to be sung, because I'd not had time to rehearse. Naturally, I was very worried at the prospect of going on 'cold', but Hansi reassured me. 'Oh don't worry about it,' he said. 'You'll soon pick it up. You know the songs and I know you will do your best when you get out there. You'll be fine.' But that's his attitude.

"Sure enough he was right – and everything *did* work out well in the end, but I know a lot of other people who would rehearse you into the ground so that when the time comes for you to do the show, you are bored stiff with the programme. By not over-rehearsing his musicians, Hansi ensures the whole act stays fresh and vibrant and everyone enjoys the music they are playing. It's a good point."

Since that first engagement, Madeline Bell has become a vital part of the orchestra adding her own superb vocal range to many of Last's exciting arrangements.

"I must say that I do like the music he plays," she says. "Although I don't always like his arrangements. But that's just professional rivalry. Somebody asked me when I was hosting my own Radio One Sunday morning

show why I didn't play James Last records on the programme. So I told them the truth. Hansi plays cover versions, re-arrangements of hit songs and that's really what he does so well, and the music is excellent. But I would rather play the originals.

"People have often tried to analyse Hansi's success, but to me the answer is quite simple. He gives the average hard working man – I wouldn't want to put any class on it because he gets all kinds of people in his audiences from eight to eighty – what he wants to hear.

"At a James Last concert, you'll find everyday people in the audience, the rich, the poor and the famous. And when they go to a show, they want to hear the songs they know. Hansi gives them just that, nothing pretentious. He doesn't start experimenting with new material, just plays it straight down the line. He knows his audience and caters exclusively for it. That's why he rarely puts in any of his own material, even though he is a great writer and has written some superb songs. But when you're on to a winner, you stick with it, especially in this business. He does manage to get a couple of tracks of his own on to his albums, but usually he stays faithful to his tried and tested formula of playing covers of old hits, or what I call rejuvenations of standards.

"And he's doing just fine."

Drummer Barry Reeves is a veteran member of the James Last Orchestra, having joined in 1971 and later replacing Hansi's brother Robert, who left to form his own band.

Born in Birmingham, Barry started his musical career working with various local British rock groups before he went to Germany to record with Les Humph-ries. He liked the country so much that he decided to stay, and later moved into session work in Hamburg. It was while working as a drummer in the studios, that he was asked to sit in with the Last Orchestra.

"I got booked to play the percussion parts on that first session," he says. "It was not the actual drumming part, more what we call in the business . . . playing with the toys.

"We were working on a number for a television show and had to play *Blacksmith Blues*. All I had to do was bang two metal blocks together in time to the music. Throughout the entire number, my job was to bang out the tempo using these odd-looking instruments. But I did actually get to play an eight bar solo in the middle!

"I think Hansi just wanted to test me out and to see how good I was at keeping time. After completing the track, he came up to me and asked me if I'd like to join the band. It was as simple as that, quite ridiculous really. Then he asked me if I could play tambourine and I said, 'yes, I suppose so'. And that was it . . . very casual and matter of fact.

"Since then I've toured the world with the band and had a ball."

Having worked with James Last now for over a dozen years, Barry has come to know the man better than most. He, too, is a member of his fan club.

"He's a fantastic man," he adds. "I've known him for so long that our friendship is more like a father and son relationship. I'm very close to the family – and they are all such marvellous people. Success hasn't affected him one little bit. He treats all the musicians superbly well, but if you ask any member of the orchestra the

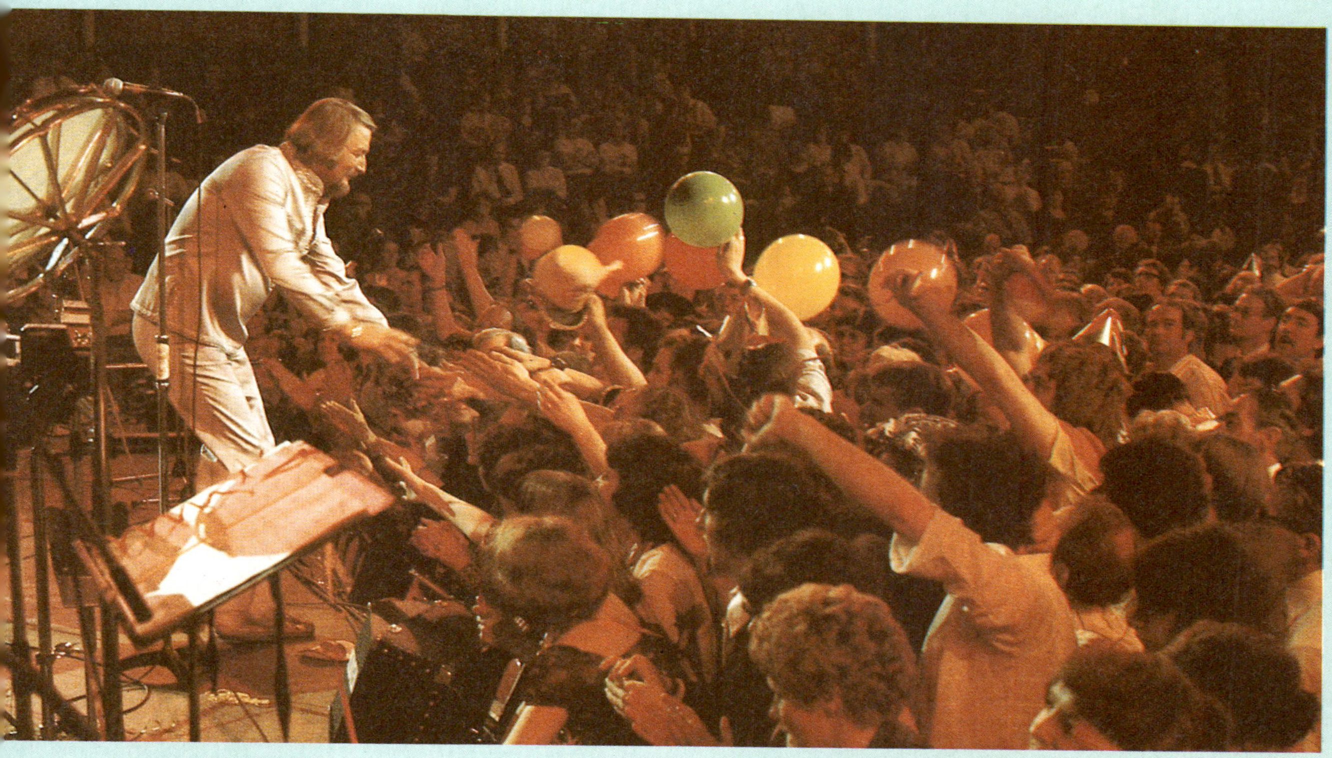

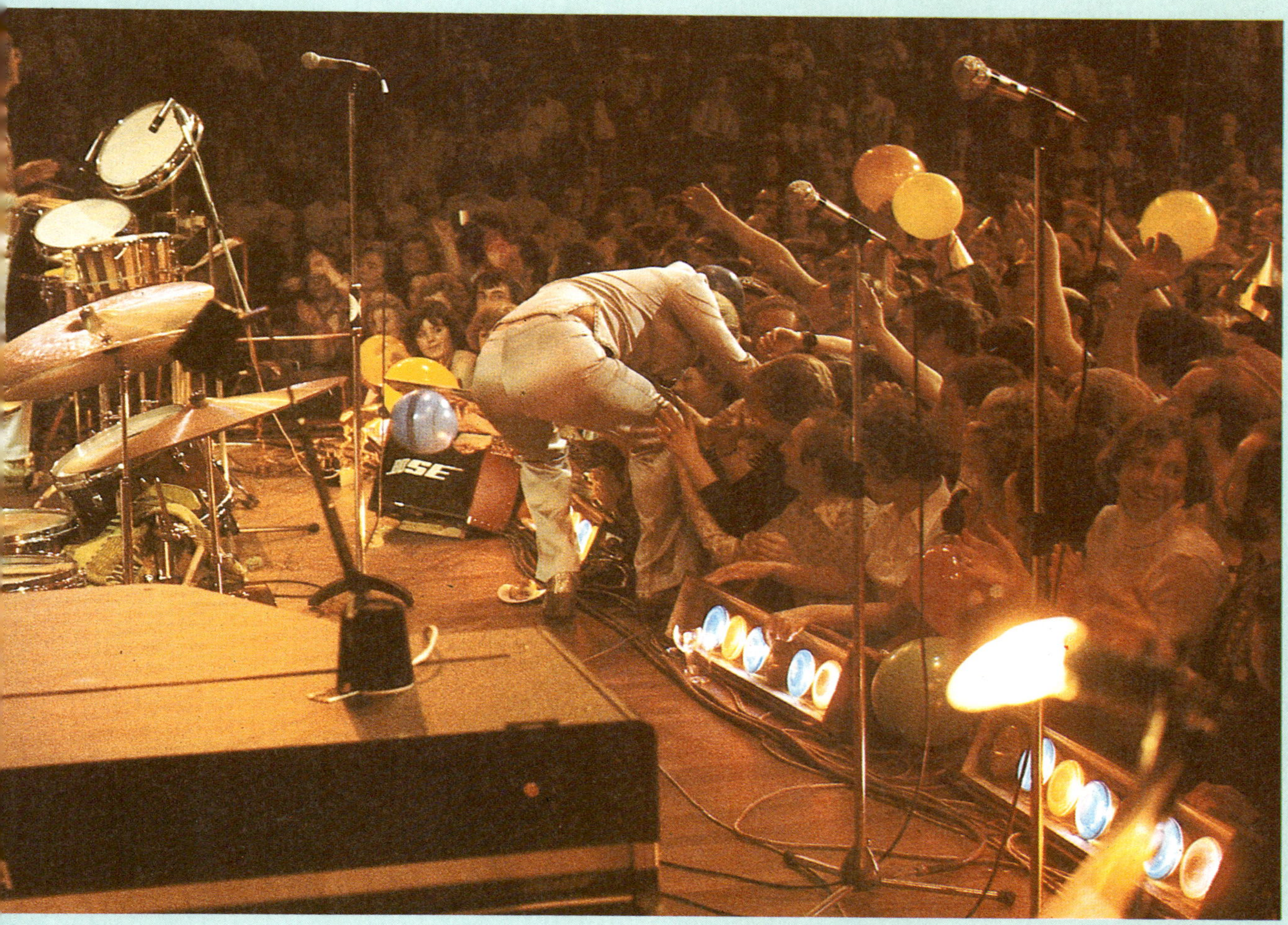

same question, they'll give you exactly the same reply.

"Hansi's very fond of his musicians and he makes it his job to find out if there are any personal problems as well as what's going on. Being a former band member, and having worked hard for a long time before he finally made a success for himself, he understands the problems of musicians. He knows what they like and what they dislike. He knows, too, what makes them happy and what upsets them.

"People have often said that he works us hard when we're on the road, but when you work with Hansi, you know what to expect from him. He's *not* a hard task master. Doesn't have to be, he knows what he wants, and he gets it because everybody respects him, we'll do anything for him. He pays us well, too, but that's not the point. I think we'd all work for him for nothing if it came to the crunch – he's that kind of person.

"Hansi likes to be totally involved with his musicians. He works with them and likes to relax with them. He also makes life easy for them when he's out on tour and can't do enough for them. All the little things that add up.

"When we're out on the road, Hansi will always see to it that there is a bar and a buffet laid on for us after every single concert. Even at sound checks and rehearsals, there is always something to eat and drink on hand for the lads and the dressing room is always well supplied with drinks. That's something you rarely find with other artists. I've worked on several rock tours where nothing like that has happened."

Being one of the old men of the James Last Orchestra, in terms of length of service, of course, Barry has witnessed several changes over the years.

"When I joined the orchestra," he says, "it was just like a typical German oompah band. But over the years, it has developed magnificently. Hansi is always on the look out for new ideas and techniques, and he spent two years in America not long ago trying to come up with something new. Looking for a new form of creativity.

"In the past, people have often knocked him for being uncreative, but they don't know the man, and they certainly don't realise that his arrangements only add to the music he is playing. Let's face it, James Last can never become stale because he has a wealth of music, from all over the world, to call upon. He can't possibly run out of material and from what I can see, he'll never run out of ideas for arrangements, either. He doesn't need to change his style – up-date it occasionally, sure – change it, never.

"Hansi hit upon the idea of rejuvenating pop songs in his own style, first. It was his idea and he has become outstandingly successful at doing it, so much so that many other people tried to copy him over the years. But *they* failed because Hansi was the first. The original . . . and the best.

"Once his idea took off, however, it went like a rocket. The rocket's still soaring.

"One thing that hasn't changed in all the time I've been with the band, however, is the fans. They have remained constant. I would hate to label them, they are just normal, every day people, who like to enjoy themselves with Hansi's party music. Instead of sitting at home in front of the television every night, they like to have fun and a good time. They certainly let their hair down at concerts, it's beautiful to see and brings tears to my eyes. The people go absolutely wild, especially in England and Japan, but even Hansi can't really understand why his music has been so successful and caused such a reaction. He can't really believe it's happening."

One of the highspots in the James Last year comes in January with the annual knees up party in the Ernst-Merck Halle in Hamburg. The James Last Carnival, and Barry Reeves has played at them all.

"They are mad, zany, crazy affairs," he says. But, wow, what great fun, everyone goes absolutely wild. The party lasts for two days solid, non-stop dancing virtually around the clock, although they do try to close them down at six in the morning, and open the doors again at six the following evening. Usually, there is a swop over band like Acker Bilk to ring the changes of musical styles, and selected guest artists. But there is a tremendous carnival atmosphere inside the hall and we all enjoy playing at them immensely. Anything and everything goes, and people dress up in the most weird and wonderful costumes. It's amazing, and the audiences really enter into the spirit of the occasion.

"But I've seen sights similar to Hamburg all over the place on my travels. It doesn't matter where we are, Hansi seems to have the same affect on people. He generates so much love and happiness. It's the same the whole world over."

When Barry talks about James Last, his eyes light up and you can see just how much fun and enjoyment he has had with the band over the years. It's written all over his face. He grins as he remembers new stories, and speaks reams of the admiration and affection he has for

the entire Last family. You get the feeling that even the bad times have been marvellous. The good times have been a joy.

"I can remember one lovely incident," he says, and his face instantly cracks into a hearty smile. "I went round to Hansi's house one night just as he and Waltraud were preparing to go out for the evening to the Press Ball at the Atlantic Hotel in Hamburg. I had only called on the off chance of seeing them both, but Hansi asked if I would go along with them.

"Well, I couldn't possibly join them because for a start, I wasn't properly dressed. I was only wearing jeans and an old shirt. So how could I go to a prestigious occasion like that? But Hansi and Waltraud insisted and then set about finding me some suitable clothes to wear.

"Within minutes, they had solved the problem and come up with a perfect answer. I wore one of Hansi's shirts and ties, Waltraud's jacket, their son Ronny's trousers – he was only twelve at that time, but even then he was bigger than I was – and their daughter Caterina's shoes. Then, all dressed up and looking rather splendid even if I say so myself, I escorted Mr. and Mrs. Last to the ball. If only the people there had known what I was really wearing . . ."

David Martin is today one of the finest songwriters Britain has produced with a string of hit songs to his credit, including *Can't Smile Without You* which was recorded by Barry Manilow in 1979 and *There's A Whole Lot Of Loving*, a number Guys And Dolls took to the top of hit parades all over the world in 1975.

In a career spanning twenty years in showbusiness, David has written material for Elvis Presley, David Essex, Andy Williams, Engelbert Humperdinck, and The Carpenters. Yet coupled with an outstanding ability to write hit records, is an accomplished voice. For many years, David was a member of an elite band of British session singers whose vocal talents enhanced many dozens of international hits.

For four years, between 1977 and 1981, he was also a part of the James Last Orchestra and recorded extensively with the band and undertook several tours.

Being a highly-talented musician in his own right, adept also at arranging and producing, Martin is an ideal person to assess the unique qualities that James Last possesses. He does it willingly.

"James Last is a very talented and accomplished man," says David. "He's a unique man and a brilliant musician. Professionally speaking, there is none finer. He can take what are basically old songs – whether they are Top Ten hits, classics, Russian folk songs, calypsos, whatever – and turn them into something very special indeed. He gets a sound and a treatment that to me is totally original. He breathes new life into songs and he does it so cleverly. But then, Hansi is a very clever man and very perceptive.

"There's an aura about him, a tremendous warmth and presence which comes over on his records, *and* comes across the stage when he's performing live. He only has to stand there out in the spotlight and conduct the orchestra, and a fantastic magic radiates from him. It's called charisma.

"Personally speaking, Hansi is one of the most generous and kind-hearted people I have ever met. He's generous to a fault, and that comes over in the way he treats everyone who becomes involved with him. As you know, Hansi has his big happy family, and he looks after it.

"Actually, his goodnaturedness can sometimes become embarrassing, and I mean that in the nicest possible way.

"People have told you stories of his treatment of the band, how he lays on meals for them after the show. But it goes a lot further than that.

"If you happen to be in an hotel dining room, eating breakfast, and Hansi is sitting near to your table, he'll pay the bill for you without any fuss or ado. When the time comes to settle up with the waiters chances are Hansi has picked up the tab. He's an amazing bloke. It gets to the point that you don't want to sit close to him at meal time in case he feels you're taking advantage of him. Quite honestly, though, I don't think the thought would ever enter his head."

For one so closely involved with all aspects of the recording industry and highly successful at that, David Martin has his own views on the real secret of Hansi's amazing success.

"I've been trying to fathom it out for years," he says, "and of course, *talent* is the vital ingredient. Hansi has talent in abundance. But he's also a very shrewd operator.

"Whenever he goes out on tour, he does his homework to perfection. When he is given the itinerary of engagements, he will make sure that the programme for each concert is personalised for each and every audience. If he goes to Ireland, he will adapt his programme to include songs like *Danny Boy* and a few Irish jigs. In Australia, *Waltzing Matilda* will appear. In Japan, there will be a certain section devoted to local ethnic

james last

Für mehr als 100.000 in den Niederlanden verkaufte Tonträger
"IN CONCERT"

POLYDOR B.V.   Rijswijk, den 18. Februar 1980

music. In England, he'll put in a traditional sing-along section. Nothing is too much trouble for him and he works his arrangements around the songs. Naturally, the audiences love him for his dedication. He is totally popular and gets to the hearts of the people by giving them what they want to hear. He creates atmosphere on record and in concert, and I think basically that is exactly what he set out to do in the first place. It works well and when you are part of the family set up, you get swallowed up in that atmosphere, and it inspires you to greatness. That atmosphere bounces back off the audience, too, and that's a very special quality to possess. Whether you like him or loathe him, you can't help but admire the man. I think he's the greatest.''

David actually joined the James Last Orchestra almost by accident, during one of the most creative and successful periods of his entire career.

''I'd always been involved with singing and song-writing and for several years, as a session singer, I'd worked with Sue Glover, and Sunny Leslie, and Tony Burrows who had all been members of the James Last Choir for quite a long time. We appeared on many major hit records together as back-up singers and we estimated that at one time, we had been responsible – indirectly, of course – for selling over 25,000,000 records around the world. We had also put out a few records of our own under various different stage names.

''As you can imagine, it can be very frustrating when you see a record you helped to create reach the top of the charts and you don't even get a credit for your contribution to its success.

''In 1977, however, I wrote a song called *First Night* and instead of putting it out for offers for other artists to cover, I called Sue, Sunny and Tony and suggested to them that it would be a great idea if we recorded the song ourselves, using the name Original Cast. They agreed and, shortly afterwards, the record was released.

''At that time, there was a James Last concert tour of Britain in the pipeline and the three other singers said they would approach Hansi to see if he would let us sing the song on stage with him during the course of the tour. It wasn't a bad idea, but there was a problem. Although they had been long established members of his orchestra, I didn't know the man at all and I was very worried how he would react to the inclusion of a stranger.

''The next thing I knew, however, was that the girls had played the record to Hansi during a recording session in Hamburg, and he wanted to meet me. Would I go over and sit in on a session? I jumped at the opportunity of working with the great man. Tony and the girls had told me all about him and what a fabulous person he was, so I was highly flattered at the invitation. And when we met, everything the others had told me was true. 'Sure you can sing your song,' he said, and then out of the blue, he asked me to join the Choir. That was it . . . it was a pure chance, and I accepted immediately.

''Quite honestly, it was the best decision I ever made and they were the most remarkable four years I ever spent.''

David left the band in 1981, but it was a difficult decision to make.

He adds: ''I have always been very actively involved in the music industry in my own right, either as a singer, writer, producer or arranger, and I suppose after I'd spent a few years on the road and in the studio with James Last, I got itchy feet. I had stopped doing a lot of studio work on my own to concentrate on my career with Hansi. But by 1981 I decided the time was right to start getting involved for myself once again.

''During my four years with the orchestra, I had still managed to write songs. In 1978 and 1979 I was lucky enough to have three songs in the finals of the World Popular Song Festival in Tokyo. One of them – *You* – won the Most Outstanding Song Award, which was fantastic. And in 1980, Madeline Bell and I recorded another of my compositions, *Together Again*, which also proved a great success. So I was still pretty active. But I did feel that I couldn't really concentrate my attention on two totally separate careers.

''I desperately wanted to return to doing my own thing, and after I formed my own recording company – Deb Records – I determined that the time was right to part company with Hansi and the band. It was a hard decision to make and I was terribly reluctant about leaving.

''Still nobody said that I was sacked . . . and I don't even feel as if I have left the group. I'm still very close to Hansi and all the musicians. And who knows, maybe I might tour again with them in the future.

''I do know one thing, though. I'm sure that if I rang him up and asked for my old job back, he'd say come along. That's the kind of bloke he is. And I feel proud to have been associated with him.

''Once you have been a member of the James Last Family – you are always a member. It's an exclusive club, presided over by the most amazing man in the world . . . James Last.''

Enough said.

HANSIMANIA

POLYSTAR POL VM 14

*t*HERE ARE VERY FEW PEOPLE IN THIS WORLD WHO can number their friends in *millions*.

James Last can.

And his friends cover all nationalities and creeds, all colours and ages.

Last's friends are simply the millions of people who buy his records avidly. The thousands of people who go to see him perform live with incredible regularity. The hundreds who stop him in the street to chat about the latest recording session.

Hansi has a very special relationship with his fans. He lays on lavish parties for them and likes to meet as many of them as he possibly can. Unlike many of his superstar contemporaries, James Last goes out of his way to make contact . . . and involves himself with their lives. It's never too much trouble, there is always time, even during the most hectic schedule.

"Hansi has a very personal relationship with his fans," says Peter Boosey, secretary of the James Last World Wide Appreciation Society. "He'd like to get to know them all individually if he possibly could, but then that's the kind of man he is. He's so modest and unassuming, that I don't think he can really believe he has so many friends and followers. He treasures them all."

Peter Boosey could well be described as James Last's Number One fan and a superfan at that. What he doesn't know about James Last and his music isn't really worth knowing. He can reel off facts and figures about the man like a machine gun firing tracer bullets. Ask him if Hansi has recorded a specific number, and he'll not only tell you the album it is on, he'll tell you the number, the date of release *and* the exact number of records sold. He also compiles the most detailed discographies and chart files on Last's records for the growing army of Appreciation Society members – and keeps the fans bang up to date with their idol's movements and news on forthcoming tours and record availabilities. Boosey is like a walking, talking computer on Last with a file bank mind stored with marvellous information. Indeed, one international recording company paid him the highest compliment recently, by asking him to compile sleeve note information for a box-set of James

Last records they were about to put on the market. They had been referred to Peter Boosey by Hansi's German record company, such is the high esteem Polydor hold him in.

He talks lovingly about the man, too, and his music he first encountered in 1966 at a cost of just twelve shillings and sixpence (62½p).

"When I first started buying records, I went after albums by Herb Alpert, Ray Conniff and Bert Kaempfert," he says. "But then I was introduced to a sampler LP – *This Is James Last* – which cost just twelve-and-sixpence. Being a Hi-Fi record collector, I couldn't really go wrong for that money, so I bought it. I figured that if I didn't like the album, I could always give it to my father-in-law for a Christmas present, or something like that.

"But when I first heard the LP I discovered a brand new sound. It was a fairly brassy sound – which was to my liking – but it also had a beat. Up until then, too many of the orchestras I had been listening to, were a little flat. This one was different. There was a pop group rhythm section to enhance the brass, and that's what really appealed.

"James Last was refreshingly new. I'd always liked a lot of instrumental pop records, but I was never too keen on Mick Jagger even though I must admit to liking some of the material The Stones played. Suddenly, James Last was playing this kind of pop music, but with trumpets and saxophones taking the lead instead of voices. That's what turned me.

"That first sampler sold 400,000 copies in this country, so there must have been a lot of other people in the same boat as me who discovered his music for the first time then. You could speak to a lot of other fans and you would get exactly the same story.

"*This Is James Last* was released in 1965 and started to make an impact at the beginning of the next year. Shortly afterwards, during the middle of 1966, Hansi had no less than four LP's in the British Album chart even though he was virtually unknown in England. You must remember, too, that this was at the height of The Beatles' and The Stones' popularity, so it was quite an achievement for an orchestra. But overnight, Last seemed to awaken a whole generation of British record-buyers who could at last identify themselves with somebody they liked. For the first time, somebody was catering for their listening needs.

"After that, I discovered the latest James Last album contained two or three tracks that Bert Kaempfert or Ray Conniff had already introduced to their LP's. But somehow James Last's arrangements, and his overall approach were far superior to these others. His music seemed fresher, more appealing. It was a cleaner, more modern style. Ray Conniff records were really all too similar; Bert Kaempfert's bored you after a while because there wasn't the variation in the music that Last had developed. In the end I couldn't wait for the next James Last album to be released in Britain. The other orchestras went by the board.

"A couple of years later, I had built up quite a collection, too, of maybe thirty or forty albums, before I discovered to my delight, that there was a lot more James Last material on the market, which hadn't been issued in Britain and was only available in Europe. So I made it my job to track these albums down, and I visited the Continent regularly.

"The first time, I went to Rotterdam in Holland and spent one Saturday morning searching through record stores. I managed to find over a dozen new albums that were unheard of back home, and brought them back with me. The next time, I visited Ostende in Belgium and the same thing happened. In the end, I was visiting Europe virtually once every two or three months in my quest for new material — and I even travelled as far as Basle in Switzerland for new material. Obviously somewhere along the way, I got the bug.

"As Hansi's output of albums increased and he turned that marvellous sound of his to update the classics, followed by his A-Gogo series and so on, there was so much variation in his music, that I didn't have a great deal of time to listen to anyone else. It's been like that ever since. These days, there is so much material available that the variation is fantastic. Now he is experimenting with new sounds, using synthesisers and electronic music, and recording more and more of his own, self-written music on albums. So the future looks to be very exciting. Even after seventeen years, there is a brand new sound emerging from James Last."

Peter Boosey is the first to admit that during the early days, however, the James Last sound completely dominated his life.

"I wanted to get hold of everything James Last had ever recorded. It became an obsession," he says, "although the first few issues had been put out under his real name of Hans Last, before the record company changed it.

"On my many travels through Europe, I managed to get them all, apart from the first record he ever made and I've never managed to track that one down. But I'm ever hopeful. The album is called *Die Gabs Nur Einmal* and it's a sort of German *Sing Something Simple* compilation. Somebody did, however, find me a copy tape of the songs, but I'm still determined to find the original. It's nearly twenty years old now. If I do end up finding it, I'll probably only play it once and then put it away. But it will complete my collection.

"It's funny, but collecting Hansi's records has become a mania for many James Last fans. It can get out of hand. I've come across many fans who collect the covers of his albums like postage stamps. They buy everything that is released on Hansi, even if it's the same album, but issued under a different cover! That's how dedicated they have become.

"I must admit that on one particular album — it's called *Non-Stop Dancing 1979* — I've got *thirteen* copies, and they are all different. I've got pressings from Malaya, the Philippines, New Zealand and a few more besides. The picture on the cover is identical on every copy. The tracks are the same, too, but right down at the bottom of the cover is a line of copy which reads . . . 'Made in New Zealand', or 'Made in Malaya', and each one is individual.

"Hansi has made over two hundred records during his career and I've got 2020 of them, simply because I collect all the different versions, all the different covers. I've got six or seven different copies of albums which are only slightly different from each other. I think that's what's called going over the top."

So just why is James Last so special to Peter and the millions of fans who almost worship him?

"His music has an appeal across the board," he says. "It covers every age group and his strength lies in his powerful arrangements.

"Most of his albums fall into the so-called middle of the road category that appeals to an age span of thirty to sixty-five, and there is something in that huge repertoire that appeals to everyone, and suits their particular needs. In our fan club magazines that are issued to each member of the Appreciation Society, we run a regular feature which allows the fans to choose their all-time favourite James Last tracks. And you would be surprised at the variation in their likes and dislikes. No two fans like the same thing. Some go for the classical material, others choose the A-Go go series, or the Beach Party albums, while others plump for the modern music.

Yet the common denominator all the time, is Hansi himself . . . and that just shows his remarkable versatility. He caters for so many people's tastes.

"Hansi also creates a marvellous atmosphere on record. It's happy-go-lucky music, without heavy messages . . . just good professional fun.

"It's funny, but Hansi has been conscious of the fact that his fans in Britain have always been slightly older than those in Europe and he has often wondered why the young people of this country don't go to his concerts or buy his records. I believe that the fault lies with the media in Britain, they have been responsible for driving many of the young people away.

"If you listen to the domestic radio programmes these days, the presenters tend to play James Last material that dates back to the late 1960's, and they feature the same records time and time again. So that when people listen to a particular song you can imagine them saying – 'oh, no not that again' – and it puts them off. Chances are that something from his new albums will never be played on the air. Unfortunately, British radio, and many of the newspapers, have labelled Hansi for easy listening *only* and young people aren't into that. Yet if they were to see one of his concerts, I'm sure they would be converted.

"I get very annoyed when I read in the newspapers that James Last is dubbed as 'The King Of Corn' and his music is dismissed out of hand as 'wall-paper music', simply because I know no-one has taken the trouble to listen to it properly. The media criticise him out of hand and have created this image of schmaltz. By doing that, they are also decrying so many people who get great satisfaction from Last's albums, and intimating that there are 'morons'. That's wrong. The Press fail to notice that the man has sold nearly 60,000,000 albums around the world and become a phenomenon. The trouble is, British newspapers tend to send their rock writers to review his concerts, and they have already formed their opinions before they've heard a single note of music played. When their column appears, it is bound to be derogatory towards the man. It has happened so many times in the past, that it's unbelievable. It gives him a very bad name and no wonder people who haven't experienced his music, cringe at the mere mention of his name.

"I could make up a tape of James Last music and if it was given an airing at peak-listening time on the radio, it would probably win Hansi another two million fans. I could pick some of his more progressive material which the young people couldn't possibly have heard, or wouldn't even contemplate listening to, because it says 'James Last' on the cover, and I guarantee they would enjoy it."

Strong words, but Boosey knows what he's talking about. He started the James Last World Wide Appreciation Society in 1974, and it has been his life and a labour of love ever since.

"When I started chasing around Europe, looking for new records, I also started writing to Polydor – his record company – for any information on Hansi. Actually, at that time there wasn't very much material available," he says. "But they used to reply to my letters, enclosing news on his latest album releases.

"Then one day during a British concert tour, I wrote to the company again and told them that I was going to see one of the concerts at the Albert Hall and asked if there was any possibility that I might meet James Last. His A & R manager replied, and actually sent me a backstage pass, admitting me behind the scenes. I couldn't believe it.

"So on the night in question, I nipped backstage, showed my pass and introduced myself to Hansi. I told him that I believed I was his Number One fan in Britain and that I possessed every album he had ever made, except one. He was a lovely man and we had a marvellous chat about his music. Then he took the time and trouble to introduce me to all his musicians. It was a fabulous experience for me.

"The next night, so I have been told, one of the Polydor executives went along to see Hansi and to find out what *he* thought of me. At that time, the record company was thinking of starting an Appreciation Society. They knew all about me through my letters and obviously I appeared to be the most fanatical fan in Britain – though I wouldn't have said that knowing some of the people I know today. I think Polydor were impressed by my enthusiasm and the fact that I went to such lengths to get James Last's records.

"Hansi must have liked me as well, because the next thing that happened was the record company contacted me and asked if I would like to start the fan club. Polydor supplied me with about eight thousand names of fans they had kept on file . . . and we took it from there. Our initial membership was about five hundred people. Since then, we have attracted over six thousand.

'I was flattered to be asked to start the club, because it was common knowledge in Germany that James Last was *against* such an idea there. The Germans tend to regionalise the operations. Very quickly, he could see a James Last Appreciation Society springing up in Frankfurt, then one in Hamburg, another in Bonn and he didn't like the idea. He realised that it would have put such a great demand on his administration that the clubs would have been impossible to run successfully. Hansi didn't want that to happen. When Polydor said they should start one in Britain, they obviously told James Last that it would be run on a national basis – one club, one secretary – and Hansi was delighted."

Peter Boosey was born in Tilbury in Essex, in 1941, and started his professional working career in the engineering section of the British Bata Shoe Company. During his spare time, he became very actively involved in local pop groups, and managed several. In one group under his charge – The Palaminos – there was a young up and coming singer by the name of Paul Raven who was later to change his name to . . . Gary Glitter.

In 1962, the group undertook a series of engagements in Germany, minus the yet-to-become Glitter, who claimed there wasn't enough money in the booking for him. So he opted out. But as manager to the boys, Peter thought it was only right that he accompany them

to Germany, and everyone thought that they were on the verge of a great success.

Unfortunately, they didn't quite make it to the top, and later disbanded. Peter, however, persevered and by the mid 60's found himself booking various groups into a number of small clubs in and around the Essex area and several United States Airforce bases up and down the country.

"Not long afterwards, The Rolling Stones arrived on the scene with a bang," he says. "The clubs I was supplying with groups expected the bands to appear smartly dressed on stage, wearing suits. But with the Stones-boom, jeans and T-shirts became the order of the day as standard group uniform and many of my groups refused to wear suits. Naturally, the clubs involved decided to look elsewhere for their entertainment needs."

So Peter decided to quit the group scene and turned his hand to becoming a disc jockey.

"I was still working at Bata's by day, and my DJ work was confined to semi-professional activities," he adds. "But I spent most of my weekends playing the Top Ten hits in many of the clubs I had once booked. By now I had become hooked on James Last's music, so many of the records I featured during my act were by Hansi himself . . . and they went down very well indeed. Before long I'd built up quite a reputation for myself. Club audiences liked my musical tastes and wanted to book me.

"At the same time, through the Appreciation Society, I started a small, part-time record business, supplying James Last material to the fans. By 1978 business was doing so well that I decided it was time to start up on my own. Since then I've combined my time running a successful James Last Appreciation Society and my own business. Both work hand in hand.

"If a James Last album is released in England, I have usually sold between six and seven hundred of them to fans even before the record hits the shops. The fans don't like to wait for new material. So we also started importing other material from abroad which we offered to the members on mail order. Things just snowballed from there and before long, I was getting enquiries from shops to supply *their* James Last records. Today, I suppose, I supply records to nearly a hundred outlets."

Since 1974, however, the James Last World Wide Appreciation Society has flourished. From humble beginnings, it has developed into one of the best organised fan clubs in the business, through Peter Boosey's sheer dedication and hard work. It seems he has inherited a fine legacy from his musical mentor. Today, the club provides a marvellous service for its members – and Peter personally writes, produces and publishes a delightful, glossy fan magazine six times a year, for which he also takes most of the photographs. That's not all . . . he organises special events for the Society which range from full scale holidays in Spain, to visits to the James Last Carnivals in Hamburg; party evenings; weekends away and local discos. It is proving to be a full-time job.

Says Peter: "My wife Pamela helps me with the record business, but ninety per cent of her time is tied up with administration for the Society. And I have to employ another lady who comes in to help out, but most of *her* work is taken up with the fan club as well. When you think that we have to distribute six thousand magazines every two months, it is becoming a full-time occupation. But we don't mind at all . . . James Last is worth it.

"During 1982, we also organised Hansi discos all over Britain, which were publicised through the magazine. I suppose we held thirty such events throughout the year with Yours Truly acting as the host and disc jockey.

"But that's just a small part of our organisation. We have also run several more lengthy trips to the Continent to see the James Last Orchestra, and each time we go over to Europe, Hansi makes a special effort to see us and say 'hello'.

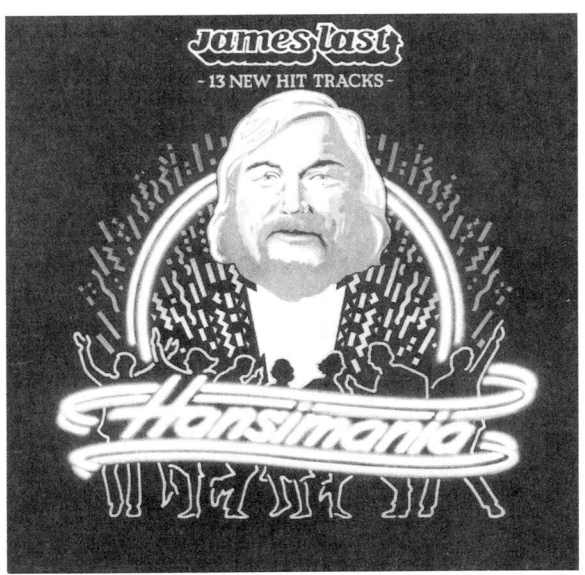

"In March 1981 we set up a trip for a hundred and fifty members to visit Bremen for a concert appearance. James Last had a very tight schedule on that evening, he was moving the orchestra on to another destination immediately the show was completed. Still, during the concert, he took the trouble to introduce the English contingent to the audience, and afterwards, he came on to our coaches and thanked everyone personally for coming. He loves this personal contact.

"Every year when we organise visits to Hamburg for the James Last party evenings, Hansi *always* meets us personally on our arrival and looks after us. In 1982, four hundred English fans made the trip, and Hansi took us all to an old Holsten Brewer House restaurant and beer cellar where he treated us to lunch and then entertained us for the afternoon. Once before, he hired the town hall and laid on a marvellous meal. Another year, when we arrived in Hamburg, he greeted us with a full-scale oompah band *and* his own orchestra were there on the platform playing away as our train pulled into Hamburg station!

"1982 proved to be a very hectic year for the Appreciation Society, with trips to Bremen, Copenhagen and Aachen to see Hansi performing. We were also planning a trip to Toronto in the spring to coincide with Hansi's Canadian tour, and at one stage two hundred members were going along. But the tour was unfortunately cancelled. Still, we hope to complete the visit in 1983!

"So there is always plenty going on. In the past, though, we made most of our arrangements through a middle agent – sometimes through Thomas Cook – but these days we do all the bookings and organisation ourselves."

One of the undoubted highlights of the year came in November when two hundred and fifty James Last fans travelled to Spain for a week-long holiday, during which time the Society took over the disco in their chosen hotel every evening and played James Last's music non-stop.

"A few years ago, we took a smaller number to Lloret De Mar," adds Peter, "and we were lucky enough to be given the disco facilities by the hotel management as a venue for us to hold our parties. At the same time, a few hundred other hotel residents were attending a dance in the ballroom upstairs and dancing to the music of a local Spanish group. The band that was playing was excellent and they catered for every musical style and taste, but they created absolutely no atmosphere in the ballroom.

"Downstairs at our disco, the party was really going with a swing. The place was bursting at the seams with everyone dancing and enjoying themselves to Hansi's music. Throughout the course of the evening, several of the people from the function upstairs came down to join in with our fun. And the same thing happened every night of our stay there.

"I actually went upstairs during one interval and bought the boys in the band a drink and they asked me *when we were going home*! They couldn't stand the competition. I think that says it all."

In the eight years or so he has been running the fan club, Peter Boosey has got to know so many different kinds of people, and you would have thought he would be the one person to best describe a typical James Last fan. But even he has difficulty.

"It is very hard to describe a typical James Last fan," he admits, for once almost lost for words. "They are all so different. They come from all walks of life, all classes, and as I said before, they all have their own favourite kinds of James Last music. But the common bond is that they love to let their hair down and appreciate Hansi's sounds.

"We have members in over forty different countries now, although we started initially for the British fans. We have members in Brazil, and most of the other English speaking countries of the world, though our range stretches to Israel, Malta, Australia, New Zealand, Zambia, the Seychelles and the Middle East. We even have one member in Afghanistan, though we haven't heard a word from him since the Russian invasion.

"When we make our pilgrimages to Hamburg each January, we meet up with our Continental members. The great thing is we now find fans in this country making new friendships with their European counterparts, and staying with each other for holidays. And just think, it was the music that brought them together in the first place.

"I really don't think, however, that there is a typical James Last fan. Everyone is an individual; they are ordinary, nice people. The majority of fans fall into an age group of thirty-five to fifty, though the eldest member in the Society is over eighty, and recently, one of our friends enrolled his new-born baby as a member. In some cases we have children of nine and ten joining the club. It takes all sorts. We have professional people, lawyers, doctors . . . and one of the people who occasionally helps me out with the club, owns his own shipping company! But then at the other end of the scale,

we have members who are factory employees, labourers and several who have been made redundant.

"So, James Last fans are hard to label, but if you were to talk to them about music, you wouldn't get the type of people who like Pink Floyd, Hendrix or Cream."

In his quest to bring the latest information and up-to-the-minute news to his members, Peter Boosey has travelled many thousands of miles with the James Last Orchestra – "because I take most of the photographs used in our magazine, and I've *got* to keep up to date, it is essential for me to keep in close contact with the musicians," he adds. "In recent years, I have toured extensively with the band. I find the best time to approach the various musicians for information, is after an evening's engagement when they are relaxing and they are more than willing to spend a few hours talking to me and posing for pictures". He has also become a great friend with the man who provided him with his initial inspiration.

"I've never met another person like James Last," he adds. "He is unique: he's a multi-millionaire and yet, he is so natural. He has so much respect for everyone he comes into contact with.

"I've never yet seen the man harrassed, and when you think that at each venue the band performs, he personally supervises the installation of all the equipment, and in particular, the gigantic 25,000 watt sound system that guarantees his perfect sound, it's unbelievable. He never gets flustered, never panics, even when things start to go wrong. If you disagree with him on a subject, he will always listen to your side of the story and will often be swayed by your argument. He also values your advice and will often seek you out to find exactly what you think on a subject.

"Not long ago, someone wrote a stinking letter to me, slating Hansi. I retaliated by writing an equally forthright reply. When James Last heard about the incident, he was very upset, and he told me that I shouldn't write back in his defence. I should bite my tongue and let him get on with it. You see, Hansi doesn't seek controversy and often his true opinion is never expressed. He's a gentleman . . . and always will be.

"His attitude to the Society and its members is tremendous. He regularly writes for the magazine, and I can't imagine there is another artist who would treat his fans the way he does.

"When I first started buying James Last records, I did so because I liked his music. I didn't know the man, and he might well have been a right so-and-so for all I was aware. Now my appreciation is just as much for the man as it is for the music.

"Hansi has always said he makes happy music – it reflects his lifestyle. I feel that if I had been the fan club secretary to any other artist, I know I would have found it very difficult to get close to the star in question and to glean the information I needed for my members. So many artists today are surrounded by middle men. They are virtually protected from their fans, and to reach them, you have to first go through an intermediary. James Last is so different.

"He's a friend."

JAMES LAST ALBUMS

(Because of Last's vast output even his record companies have difficulty keeping their catalogues up to date, but the following is the most detailed discography available.)

A DATE WITH JAMES LAST
Bacarole, Prisoners Chorus, Hungarian Dance No. 5, Waltz in A Flat Op 39 No. 15, Toreadors March, To The Spring.
Moon River, Telstar, Canadian Sunset, Patricia, Moonglow, Anna.

JAMES LAST A GOGO
My Love, Mack The Knife, Little Brown Jug, That's Life, Lara's Theme.
Fly Me To The Moon, Caravan, America, What Now My Love, Funiculi-Funicula.

JAMES LAST ALBUM
A Man And A Woman, Wheels, My Bonnie, Montego Bay, What Now My Love, Il Mondo, Winchester Cathedral, Funiculi-Funicula, Blowin In The Wind, Around The World, Guantanamera, Yesterday.

ALL ABOARD WITH CAP'N JAMES
Take Us With You Captain, Sail Again To Bombay, The Boy At The Rail, La Paloma, My Bonnie, Kari Waits For Me, The Banks Of Sacramento, What Shall We Do With The Drunken Sailor, Madagascar, The Wreck Of The John B, The Yellow Rose Of Texas, When The Ships Accordian Plays, Blonde Sailor, Accordian Joe.
A Sea Journey Is Fun, Today We Sail Away, The Way With Every Sailor, Aloha Oe, John Kanaka, Up She Goes, Rolling Home, The Winds Are Blowing, Sailing Through The Storm, The Colour Flags, Hey Hey Hey, Goodnight Ladies, In My Homeland, Must I Go.

ALREDEDOR DEL MUNDO 1
Granada, Espana, La Maleguena Salerosa, Valencia, Camino Verde, Malaguena, Cachita, Cu Cu Rru Cu Cu Paloma, Mambo No. 5, Guantanamera, Mexican Hat Dance, The Lonely Bull.

ALREDEDOR DEL MUNDO 2
Plaisir D'Amour, La Seine, Sur Les Ponts D'Avignon, Moulin Rouge, Et Maintenant, La Mer.
Canto Dei Gondolieri, Vieni Vieni, Santa Lucia, La Golondrina, Ciribiribin, Baci Al Buio.

ALWAYS
Begin The Beguine, Funiculi-Funicula, Mack The Knife, Carmen 68, La Mer, Vive L'Amour, Everybody Loves A Lover.
Hava Nagila, Bei Mir Bist Du Schon, My Bonnie, Down By The Riverside, Little Brown Jug, Always, My Guy's Come Back.

AN EVENING OUT WITH JAMES LAST
Let The Sunshine In, Maria, Moon River, Born Free, Around The World, Never On Sunday, America, Secret Love, Aint Got No, Theme From A Summer Place, A Man And A Woman, Theme From Elvira Madigan.

ANNCHEN VON THARAU
Wem Gott Will Rechte Gunst Erweisen, Ub'immer Treu Und Redlichkeit, Ein Mannlein Steht Im Walde, Sah Ein Knab' Ein Roslein Steh'n, In Einem Kuhlen Grunde, Wenn Alle Brunniein Fliessen, Du Du Liegst Mir Im Herzen, Der Mai Ist Gekommen, Das Wandern Ist Des Mullers Lust, Annchen Von Tharau, Es Zogen Drei Burschen, Lang Lang Ists Her, Muss I Denn, Madele Ruck Ruck Ruck.
Horch Was Kommt Von Draussen Rein, Der Jager Aus Kurpfalz, Freut Euch Des Lebens, Gold Und Silber Lieb' ich Sehr, Wenn Ich Ein Voglein War, Am Brunnen Vor Dem Tore, Steh'ich In Finst'rer

Mitternacht, Weisst Du Wieviel Sternlein Stehen, Nun Ade Du Mein Lieb' Heimatland, Guter Mond Du Gehs So Stille, Ich Weiss Nicht was Soll Es Bedeuten, Das Lieben Bringt Gross' Freud, Im Krug Zum Grunen Kranze, Es Klappert Die Muhle Am Rauschenden Bach.

ANNCHEN VON THARAU 2
Alle Vogel Sind Schon Da, Mit Dem Pfeil Dem Bogen, Hoch Auf Dem Gelben Wagen, Abend Wird Es Wieder, Ade Nun Zur Guten Nacht, Der Mond Ist Aufgegangen, Im Wald Und Auf Der Heide, Hinaus In Die Ferne, Es Blies Ein Jager Wohl In Sein Horn, Jetzt Gang I Ans Brunnele, Bald Gras Ich Am Neckar, Es Waren Zwei Konigskinder, Ach Wie Ists Moglich Dann, Drei Lilien Drei Lilien, Hab'mein Wagen Vollgeladen, Lippe-Detmold Eine Wunderschone Stadt, Auf Der Luneburger Heide, Sabinchen War Ein Frauenzimmer, Komm Lieber Mai Und Mache, Viel Tausend Sterne Prangen, Auf Der Schwabsche Eisebahne, Wenn Die Soldaten Durch Die Stadt, Wohlan Die Zeit Ist Kommen Rosestock Holderblut, Drunten Im Unterland, Gestern Abend Ging Ich Aus, Ich Bin Der Donktor Eisenbart, Was Kommt Dort Von Der Hoh'.

AROUND THE WORLD boxed set of three records
Granada, La Malaguena Salerosa, Valencia, Camino Verde, Malaguena. Cachita, Cu Cu Rru Cu Cu Paloma, Mambo No. 5, Guantanamera, Mexican Hat Dance, The Lonely Bull, Sabeltanz, Der Rote Sarafan, Kosaken Patrouille, Kalinka, Stenka Rasin, Schiwago Melodie.
Canton Dei Gondelieri, Vieni Vieni, Santa Lucia, La Golondrina, Ciribiribin, Baci Al Buio.
Plasir D'Amour, La Seine, Sur Les Ponts D'Avignon, Et Maintenant, La Mer.
Greensleeves, Annie Laurie, Londonderry Air, The Candlelight Waltz.

AROUND THE WORLD (JAPAN)
Individual track titles not known, but we presume the titles are taken from the three record set above.

JAMES LAST AT HIS BEST – EL CONDOR PASA
Endless Journey, The House Of The Rising Sun, The Last Guest Is Gone, El Condor Pasa, Evie, Rainy Rainy, Luciana, Andanca, Tango Regina, Ballad Of The Easy Rider, Jean, Song Of The Pearl Fisher.

JAMES LAST AT HIS BEST 2 – WHO ARE WE
Who Are We, Let It Be, Telstar, Elizabeth Serenade, I Left My Heart In San Francisco, A Whiter Shade Of Pale.
El Condor Pasa, Moulin Rouge, Canadian Sunset, Endless Journey, The House Of The Rising Sun, Theme From A Summer Place.

AUF LAST GEHTS LOS
Hier Ist Was Los, Du Sag Einfach Du, 1-2-3-4 Fire, Da Kommt Jose Der Strassen-musikant, Cany Give You Anything, Paloma Blanca, Sailing, Komm Unter Meine Decke, Das War John Nie Passiert, American Patrol, In The Mood, Wir Machen Durch Bis Morgen Fruh, Jetzt Trink'ma No. A Flascheri Wein, Griechischer Wein.
Yes Sir I Can Boogie, I'm On Fire, Morning Sky, Rock Bottom, The Pushbike Song, Tanz Bitte Noch Einmal Mit Mir, Living Next Door To Alice, Komm Trink Und Trink, La Felicidad, Fett Polka, Wien Bleibt Wien, Wochenend Und Sonnenschein, Rock Around The Clock, Hound Dog.

AUF LAST GEHTS LOS 2
Sportspalast Polka, Rosamunde, Meine Rosa Ist Aus Bohmen, It's A
Heartache, Rivers Of Babylon, Buenos Dias Argentina, Pata Pata,
Bend Me Shape Me, A Banda, Fiesta Mexicana, Adieu Mein Kneiner
Gardeoffizier, Das Ist Der Fruhling In Wien, Wohin Ist Das Alles
Wohin, Die Nacht Ist Nicht Allein Zum Sclafen Da.
Night Fever, Stayin' Alive, You're The One That I Want, Belfast, Love
Is In The Air, Tanze Samba Mit Mir, The Banks of Sacramento, My
Bonnie, Kari Waits For Me, Na Na Hey Hey Kiss Him . . . Auf Der
Mauer, Ja Ja Der Chianti Wein, Charleston, Black Bottom.

BACH TO BEATLES
Bach's Toccata & Fugue, In A Persian Market, American Patrol,
Kalinka, Bye Bye Blackbird, Down By The Riverside.
Cecilia, Knock Three Times, El Condor Pasa, How Do You Do, Let
The Sunshine In, Yesterday.

BEACH PARTY
Cecilia, Once On A Sunday Morning, Blowin In The Wind,
Kumbayah, Everybody Get Together, Brasilia.
El Condor Pasa, Washington Square, Proud Mary, John Kanaka,
Madamoiselle Ninette, Give Peace A Chance.

BEACH PARTY 2
Here Comes The Sun, South Of The Border, Power To The People,
I Am I Said, Joy To The World.
Chirpy Chirpy Cheep Cheep.
Me And You And A Dog Named Boo, Jamaica Farewell, Hot Love,
The Dock Of The Bay, On The Beach, Butterfly.

BEACH PARTY 2 (U.K. only)
As above but Music From Across The Way replaces Butterfly.
BEACH PARTY 3
Banks Of The Ohio, Holy Holy, Everybody's Everything,
Wimoweh, Put Your Hand In The Hand, Swing Low Sweet Chariot.
Song Sung Blue, Jesus Christ Superstar, How Do You Do, Amazing
Grace, Poppa Joe, Wedding Song.
BEACH PARTY 4
Interlude/Feel Alright, If You Could Read My Mind, Jenny Jenny,
Killing Me Softly, Delta Queen, I'm Just A Singer In A Rock'n Roll
Band, Walk On Water.
Ave Maria No Morro, Your So Vain, But I Can Sleep In A Park, The
Night The Lights Went Out in Georgia, Finale/Lovers Dream.
BEACH PARTY 5
High Life In The Sun, I'm A Train, Sundown, Island Of Dreams,
Seasons In The Sun, I Shall Sing.
I Believe In Music, Shangri La, Billy Don't Be A Hero, Dear Father,
Beach Boy, Spanish Eyes.

BEACH PARTY 6
I Can See Clearly Now, Dunrobins Gone, Have You Never Been
Mellow, The Boxer, The Best Of My Love, Only You Can.
Lu Le La, Silver Dagger, Guava Jelly, Freedom Day, The Night They
Drove Old Dixie Down, Sorry.

BEAT IN SWEET
I Got You Babe, Frag' Den Abenwind, Baby Don't Go, You've Lost
That Lovin' Feelin', Eve Of Destruction, Teenage Love.
Mr. Tambourine Man, Du Bist Nicht Allein, For Somebody, Like A
Rolling Stone, Du Bist Meine Liebe, Yesterday.

**BEST OF JAMES LAST – NON STOP DANCING 65/70 double
album**
I'm A Believer, Good Vibrations, Have A Drink On Me, All You
Need Is Love, She'd Rather Be With Me, Okay, Ballad Of Bonnie &
Clyde, Everybody Knows, Gimme Little Sign, Jagerlatein, Eine
Schlaflose Nacht, Gloryland, I've Gotta Get A Message To You, Hey
Jude.
Help Yourself, Mrs. Robinson, It's Time To Go, Ob La Di Ob La Da,
Chewy Chewy, Eloise, Bad Moon Rising, Always Tuesday, Give Peace
A Chance, Aquarius, Let The Sunshine In, Hare Krishna, In The
Ghetto, Don't Forget To Remember.
Na Na Hey Kiss Him Goodbye, In A Gadda Da Vida, Oh Well,
Friday On My Mind, Stop Stop Stop Stop, It's Last Time, Thank U
Very Much, Mighty Quinn, John Brown's Body, Simon Says, Mony
Mony, Yummy Yummy Yummy, Only One Woman, With A Little
Help From My Friends.
I Want To Hold Your Hand, Sie Liebt Dich, I Should Have Known
Better, Love Me Tonight, Heute So Morgen So, Starparade, Mr.
Tambourine Man, Shame And Scandal In The Family, Jack The
Ripper, San Francisco, Silence Is Golden, Ha Ha Said The Clown,
Massachusetts, Hello Goodbye.

**BEST OF JAMES LAST – NON STOP DANCING 65/70 Volume 1
(Japan)**
I'm A Believer, Good Vibrations, Have A Drink On Me, All You
Need Is Love, She'd Rather Be With Me, Okay, Ballad Of Bonnie &
Clyde, Everybody Knows, Gimme Little Sign, Jagerlatein, Eine
Schlaflose Nacht, Gloryland, I've Gotta Get A Message To You, Hey
Jude, Help Yourself, Mrs. Robinson, It's Time To Go, Ob La Di Ob La
Da, Chewy Chewy, Eloise, Bad Moon Rising, Always Tuesday, Give
Peace A Chance, Aquarius, Let The Sunshine In, Hare Krishna, In The
Ghetto, Don't Forget To Remember.

**BEST OF JAMES LAST – NON STOP DANCING 65/70 Volume 2
(Japan)**
Na Na Hey Hey Kiss Him Goodbye, In A Gadda Da Vida, Oh Well,
Friday On My Mind, Stop Stop Stop Stop, It's Last Time, Thank U
Very Much, Mighty Quinn, John Brown's Body, Simon Says, Mony
Mony, Yummy Yummy Yummy, Only One Woman, With A Little
Help From My Friends.
I Want To Hold Your Hand, Sie Liebt Dich, I Should Have Known

Better, Love Me Tonight, Heute So Morgen So, Starparade, Mr. Tambourine Man, Shame And Scandal In The Family, Jack The Ripper, San Francisco, Silence Is Golden, Ha Ha Said The Clown, Massachusetts, Hello Goodbye.

BEST OF NON STOP DANCING boxed set of three
Don't Ha Ha, Shake Hands, Can't Buy Me Love, No Reply, Kiss And Shake, Downtown, Satisfaction, Wooly Bully, Ju Ju Hand, Yesterday, Du Bist Nicht Allein, Baby Don't Go, 17 Jahr' Blondes Haar, Balla Balla.

John B, A Lovers Concerto, Yellow Submarine, Yesterday Man, Bis Morgen, With A Girl Like You, Dandy, Lemon Tree, It's Last Time, Spanish Eyes, Green Green Grass Of Home, Winchester Cathedral, Music To Watch Girls By, Lass Den Dummen Kummer.

Puppet On A String, Una Festa Sui Prati, Komm Allein, Somethin' Stupid, Meine Liebe Zu Dir, I Was Kaiser Bill's Batman, Massachusetts, Words, Jagerlatein, Eine Schlaflose Nacht, Glory Land, Delilah, Bend Me Shape Me, A Banda, Jumping Jack Flash, Harper Valley P.T.A., Help Yourself, Mrs. Robinson, It's Time To Go, Simon Says, Mony Mony, Yummy Yummy Yummy, Rock Around The Clock, Charlie Brown, When The Saints Go Marchin' In, Little Arrows, Those Were The Days, Du Musst Mit Den Wimpern Klimpern, Ob La Di Ob La Da, Chewy Chewy, Eloise, Love Me Tonight, Heute So Morgen So, Starparade, I've Got To Get A Message To You, Hey Jude, Anuschka, Abendstunde Hat Gold Im Munde, Oh Happy Day, Aquarious, Let The Sunshine In, Hare Krishna.

Ra Ta Ta, Er Hat Ein Knallrotes Gummiboot, Cecilia, Na Na Hey Hey Kiss Him Goodbye, Sugar Sugar, Gruezi Wohl Frau Stirnimsa, Raindrops Keep Fallin' On My Head, Don't Forget To Remember, Azzuro, And Now Here It Comes Again, Lily The Pink, Lieber Heute Gekusst, Er Steht Im Tor, Arrivederci Hans.

JAMES LAST BEST – NUMBER TWO
For details see James Last At His Best 1 El Condor Pasa.

JAMES LAST BEST – WHO ARE WE
For details see James Last At His Best 2 Who Are We.

JAMES LAST BITTET ZUM TANZ boxed set of three
This Is The Life For Me, I'm Off To Chez Maxim, Women Women, Vilia, You Are My Hearts Delight, Nobody Loves You As Much As I Do, Beautiful World, On My Lips Every Kiss Is Like Wine, I Love You You Love Me, Laughing Women Are Beautiful, On the Paiho, Song Of The Volga, Silent Lips, My Fair Maiden.

Smiling Happiness Of Mine, Nechiedil, The Heavens Blue I'll Get For You, In My Nest Of Heavenly Blue, I Love To Kiss Women, Now The Clouds Have Rolled Away, Stay With Me Forever, Oh Maiden My Maiden, Patiently Smiling, Love What Has Given You This Magic Power, You Alone, He Will Come, Napolitana, Zorika Come Back.

Theme From Elvira Madigan, Presto From Symphony No. 7 In A Major, Romance For Violin & Orchestra In F Major Op. 50, Impromptu No. 2 In A Flat Major Op. 142, Air From Suite No. 3 In D Major, Impromptu No. 3 In G Flat Major Op. 90.

Adagio From Piano Sonata In C Minor Op. 13, Slavonic Dance No. 10, Andante From Violin Concerto In E Minor Op. 64, Prelude No. 1, Andante From Symphony No. 5 In C Minor Op. 67, Polovtsian Dances From Prince Igor.

Deep In The Heart Of Texas, Manana, Sugarbush, Exodus, Who's Sorry Now, La Bamba, Love Is A Many Spendoured Thing, My Happiness, Rum And Coca Rola, Quando Quando, South America Take It Away, Tea For Two, Day O, Me And My Shadow, Goody Goody, Ain't She Sweet, Bei Mir Bist Du Schon, The Blacksmith Blues, Sixteen Tons, Don't Fence Me In, Night And Day, In The Mood, How High The Moon, I Left My Heart In San Francisco, Tom Dooley, Happy Days Are Here Again, Yearing, Bostella.

BRAVO double album
Secret Love, Perfidia, Drina March, Never On Sunday, Begin The Beguine, Havah Nagilah, American Patrol, Wheels, La Golondring, Skokiaan, Donkey Seranade, Happy Music.

Caravan, Delicado, Passion Flower, La Mer, Un Poco Rio, Down By The Riverside, Around The World, Kiss Me Honey Honey Kiss Me, Greensleeves, Always, Adelita, Mexico City.
2634079 Spain.

CAPTAIN JAMES AT SEVEN SEAS
Ein Morgen Im Hamburger Hafen, Hamburg Ist Ein Schones Stadtchen, Muss I Denn, Blow Ye Wind, Wo Die Nordseewellen,

Kleine Mowe Flieg Nach Helgoland, Good Morning, The Sailor Boy, Rule Britannia, Greensleeves, Auf Fahrt, Fuadach Nan Gaidheal, De Kaptn De Stuermann De Bootsmann Un Ick, When Irish Eyes Are Smiling.
All Hands On Deck, Drei Matrosen, In Portugal, Von Porto Nach Barcelona, Lady Of Spain, Carmen Marsch, Shenandoah, Sorrento, Santa Lucia, Ferry Boat Serenade, Piraus, Ein Schiff Wird Kommen, High Barbaree, Hava Nagilah.

CHRISTMAS AND JAMES LAST
Happy Christmas Everywhere, Sweeter The Bells Never Rang, Sleigh Ride To The Christmas Market, The Shepherds, O Joy Over Joy, Ave Maria, In The Cathedral.
Heidschi Bumbeidschi, Tomorrow Children Is The Day, From High Up In The Sky, Silent Night, Church Bells At Christmas Time.

CHRISTMAS CLASSICS
Ave Verum Corpus (Mozart), Concerto (Violin) No. 1 In G Minor (Bruch): Adagio, Concerto (Strings) In G Minor – Christmas Concerto (Corelli), Concerto (Strings) in C – Christmas Concerto (Manfredini): Largo, For Unto Us A Child Is Born (Bach), The Four Seasons (Vivaldi): Winter – Largo, Here I Stand At Your Cradle (Bach), Serse (Handel): Largo, Thus Loved God The World.

CHRISTMAS DANCING
Kling Glockchen Klingelingeling, Lasst Uns Froh Und Munter Sein, O Du Frohliche, Leise Rieselt Der Schnee, Schneeflockchen Weissrockchen, Auf Dem Berge Da Wehet Der Wind, Morgen Kinder Wirds Was Geben, Alle Jahre Wieder, Frohliche Weihnacht Uberall, Am Weihnachtsbaume Die Lichter Brennen, Es Ist Ein Ros Entsprungen, Ihr Kinderlein Kommet, Der Christbaum Ist Der Schonste Baum, A a a.
White Christmas, Midnight In December, Jingle Bells, Kommet Ihr Hirten, O Tannenbaum, Christnacht, Morgen Kommt Der Weihnachtsmann, Wenn Der Schnee Vom Himmel Fallt, O Wunder Uber Wunder, Susser Die Glocken Nie Klingen, In Dulci Jubilo, Joseph Lieber Joseph Mein, Schlittenfahrt Im Winterwald, Stille Nacht.

CHRISTMAS WITH JAMES LAST
For details, see Christmas And James Last

CLASSICS
Intermezzo From Cavalleria Rusticana, Scherzo From Schumann's Symphony No. 2, Largo From Double Violin Concerto, Haydn's Trumpet Concerto, March To The Scaffold From Symphonie Fantastique.
Still As The Night, Last Movement From Symphony No. 39 By Mozart In E Flat Major, Beethoven's Romance, In The Hall Of The Mountain King, Brahms 2nd Movement From Symphony No. 3 In F Major.

CLASSICS FOR DREAMING
Ballad For Adeline, Carmen: Torreadors' March, Cavalleria Rusticana: Intermezzo, Concierto De Aranjuez: Adagio, Elvira Madigan: Theme, Für Elise, Liebestraume No. 3, The Moldau, Nabucco: Chorus Of Hebrew Slaves, Prince Igor: Polvtsian Dances, Romeo And Juliet: Theme, Rondo Alla Turca, Suite No. 3: Impromptu, Symphony No. 9 – *From the New World*: Adagio, The Tales of Hoffman: Barcarolle, Traumerei.

CLASSICS UP TO DATE
Barcarole, Prisoners Chorus, Hungarian Dance No. 5, Waltz In A Flat, Toreadors March, To The Spring.
Habanera, Nocturne, Romeo & Juliet, In A Persian Market, Adagio From New World, Adagio From Violin Concerto.

CLASSICS UP TO DATE
Carmen: Habanera – Toreadors' March, Hungarian Dance No. 5, In A Persian Market, Nabucco, Chorus Of Hebrew Slaves, Nocturne, Romeo And Juliet: Theme, Symphony No. 9 – *From the New World*: Adagio, The Tales Of Hoffmann: Barcarolle, To The Spring, Violin Concerto No. 1: Adagio, Waltz In A Flat.

CLASSICS UP TO DATE (Japan)
Fur Elise, Loves Dream, Solveigs Song, Elvira Madigan, Romance In F, Firework Music.
Traumerei, In A Persian Market, Intermezzo, Toreadors March, Triestesse, Air On A G String.

CLASSICS UP TO DATE 2
Theme From Elvira Madigan, Presto From Symphony No. 7 In A

Major, Romance For Violin & Orchestra In F Major Op. 50, Impromptu No. 2 In A Flat Major Op. 142, Air From Suite No. 3 In D Major, Impromptu No. 3 In G Flat Major Op. 90.
Adagio From Piano Sonata In C Minor Op. 13, Slavonic Dance No. 10, Andante From Violin Concerto In E Minor Op. 64, Prelude No. 1, Andante From Symphony No. 5 In C Minor Op. 67, Polovtsian Dances From Prince Igor.

CLASSICS UP TO DATE 2 (Japan)
For details, see Classics Up To Date 4.

CLASSICS UP TO DATE 3
Mattinata, Fantaisie-Impromptu, Orientale, Suprise, In Mir Klingt Ein Lied, Feuerwerksmusik.
Traumerei, Liebestraum, Solveigs Lied, Slawischer Marsch, Cavatine.

CLASSICS UP TO DATE 4
One Fine Day, The Moldau, Humming Chorus, Danse Espagnole, Spring Song, Concierto De Aranjuez.
Zigeunerweisen, Adagio In G Minor, Romance In G Major, Berceuse, Pavane.

CLASSICS UP TO DATE 5
Adagio, Ballade Pour Adeline, Chanson Triste, Concerto In F, Jog Din Oas, Largo, Nocturnes: Op. 27, No. 2, Op. 37, No. 2, Notre Dame: Intermezzo, Piece No. 1, Romance, Sonata No. 3.

CONCERT SUCCESSEN
Elvira Madigan, Die Moldau, Traumerei, Fur Elise, Eines Tages Sehen Wir, Intermezzo, Romance In F, Waltz In A Flat.
Andante, Berceuse, Prisoners Choir From Nabucco, In Mir Klingt Ein Lied, Concierto De Aranjuez, Liebestraum, Adagio In G Moll, Fruhlingslied.

COPACABANA – Happy Dancing
Avalon, Caminito, Chili Con Carne, El Choclo, Copacabana, Feels So Good, A Gay Ranchero, Perhaps, Perhaps, Perhaps, El Rancho Grande, Siesta, Sly Mongoose, La Sorella, Zip-a-dee-doo-dah.

COUNTRY AND SQUARE DANCE PARTY
Orange Blossom Special, Irish Washerwoman, Gary Owen, Paddy Whack, Rhinestone Cowboy, Boil Them Cabbage Down, Oh Susanna, Shenandoah, Larry O Gaff, Fire On The Mountain.
Chicken Reel, Turkey In The Straw, Dixie, Sunshine On The Mountain, Soldiers Joy, Jinrikisha, Loro Moira's, Amazon, Go Tell It On The Mountain.

DAS WUNSCHITONZERT
Prisoners Chorus, In The Hall Of The Mountain King, Tritsch Tratsch Polka, Firework Music, Toccata & Fugue.
Conversation, Fur Elise, Going Home, Hungarian Dance No. 5, Slavonic March.
Elvira Madigan, Fantasy Impromptu, Liebestraum, Ritual Fire Dance, Capriccio Italien.
Intermezzo, Tristesse, Habanera, Im Prater Bluhn Wieder Di Baume, Slavonic Dance.

DIE DREIGROSCHEN OPER
A three record set featuring Martin Held, Hannes Messemer, Achim Strietzel, Jo Herbst, Sylvia Anders, Berta Drews, F. J. Degenhardt, Hanne Wieder, Karin Ball, Harald Vock and James Last.
The complete opera.

DIE GABS NUR EINMAL
Das Gibts Nur Einmal, You Are My Lucky Star, Solang Noch Untern Lindern, Win-Wini, Tanze Mit Mir In Den Morgen, Pigalle, In Einer Kleinen Konditorei, Fraulein Pardon, Alte Kameraden, Was Kann Der Sigismund Dafur, Was Eine Frau Im Fruhling Traumt, Zwei Rote Rosen Ein Zarter Kuss, Sie Will Nicht Blumen Und Nicht Schokolade.
Schoner Gigolo Armer Gigolo, Wenn Der Weisse Flieder Wieder Bluht, Ich Kusse Ihre Hand Madame, Kalkutta Liegt Am Ganges, Du Du Du, Zuckerpuppe, Puppchen Du Bist Mein Augenstern, Mein Liebling Heisst Madi, Gluhwurchen, Wenn Die Elisabeth, Weisse Rosen Aus Athen, Ein Schiff Wird Kommen, Rosamunde, Auf Wiedersehn.

DIE GABS NUR EINMAL 2
Madonna Du Bist Schoner Als Der Sonnenschein, Sonny Boy, Es War Einmal Ein Musikus, Ist Dein Kleines Herz Fur Mich Noch Frei Baby, Ramona, Parlex Moi d'amour, True Love, Die Welt War Nie So Schon Fur Mich, Bel Ami, Ganz Paris Traumt Von Der Liebe, Jonny Wenn Du Geburtstag Hast, Bei Mir Bist Du Schon, Mister Sandman, Uber Die Prarie, Heimatios, Brazil.
Bie Dir War Es Immer So Schon, C'est Si Bon, September Song, Ich Steh'im Regen, Kosaken-patrouille, Schwarze Augen, Wolgaschiffer, Moskauer Nachte, Die Gitarre Und Das Meer, Besame Mucho, La Guitarra Brasiliana, Blue Mirage, Barcarole, Vom Stadtpark Die Laternen, So Ein Tag.

JAMES LAST DOES HIS THING
Secret Love, Kaptn James Medley, Aquarius, Rock Around With Me Medley, El Condor Pasa, Blowin' In The Wind.
Annchen Von Tharau Medley, Charmaine, Hammond A Gogo Medley, Everybody Loves A Lover.

DON'T LET THE SUN GO DOWN
The Air That I Breathe, Was Ich Sagen Will, Don't Let The Sun Go Down On Me, The Sound Of Silence, Hey Jude.
Unchained Melody, Let It Be, You Make Me Feel Brand New, A Whiter Shade Of Pale, MacArthur Park.

EAST MEETS WEST
Don't Be Sad, The Handsome Street Peddlar, Nadjenka, The Little Apple/Gapak, Samara The Beautiful City, Katjuscha/Krakowiak, The Lonely Shepherd, Trepak, Bublitschki, The Flying Troika/The Lonely Silence, The Little Bell, Kamarinskaya.
Orange Blossom Special, Irish Washerwoman, Gary Owen, Paddy Whack, Rhinestone Cowboy, Boil Them Cabbage Down, Oh Susanna, Shenandoah, Larry O Gaff, Fire On The Mountain, Chicken Reel, Turkey In The Straw, Dixie, Sunshine On The Mountain, Soldiers Joy, Jinrikisha, Loro Moiras, Amazon, Go Tell It On The Mountain.

EASY DANCING double cassette
Happy Music, Games That Lovers Play, America, That's Life, Sekai Wa Futari No Tameni, Hare Krishna, The In Crowd, Aijo, Viva L'Amour, A Man And A Woman, Baby Don't Go, Happy Heart.
Aquarius, Morgens Um Sieben Ist Die Welt Noch In Ordnung, Hemp Me Girl, Die Welt Braucht Liebe, Kiss Me Honey Honey Kiss Me, The More I See You, Let The Sunshine In, My Guy's Come Back, My Love, Delicado, Like A Rolling Stone, Teenage Love.

EL CONDOR PASA (Japan)
For details, see James Last At His Best 1 – El Condor Pasa.

EL CONDOR PASA (USA)
For details, see Beach Party.

EVERGREENS NON STOP DANCING
Deep In The Heart Of Texas, Manana, Sugarbush, Exodus, Who's Sorry Now, La Bamba, Love Is A Many Splendoured Thing, My Happiness, Rum And Coca Rola, Quando Quando, South America Take It Away, Tea For Two, Day O, Me And My Shadow, Goody Goody, Ain't She Sweet, Bei Mir Bist Du Schon, The Blacksmith Blues, Sixteen Tons, Don't Fence Me In, Night And Day, In The Mood, How High The Moon, I Left My Heart In San Francisco, Tom Dooley, Happy Days Are Here Again, Yearing, Bostella.

FANTASTIC TRUMPET
Greensleeves, Wheels, American Patrol, Never On Sunday, La Paloma, Ave Maria No Morro, Tico Tico.

La Bamba, Cherry Pink, Delicado, Passion Flower, Mexican Hat Dance, Mexico City, Granada.

FANTASTIC TRUMPET 2
Un Pocco Rio, Happy Music, Un Homme Et Une Femme, My Love, Caravan, Carmen 68, La Golondrina.
Down By The Riverside, Skokiaan, Guantanamera, Hava Nagila, La Mer, Begin The Beguine, Time After Time.

FREDDY LIVE
Freddy Quinn in concert supported by James Last.
Happy Luxemburg, Begrussungslied, In Einem Kuhlen Grunde, La Guitarra Brasiliana, Steel Guitar Rag, Tenessee Waltz, She'll Be Coming Round The Mountain, Only A Fool Like Me.
Amboss Polka, 100 Mann und ein Befehl, Spanish Eyes, Games That Lovers Play, Golden Boy, Jalisco Note Rajes, Wolga Lied, Show Me The Way To Go Home.

FREUT EUCH DES LEBENS
Fruet Euch Des Lebens, Wie Lieblich Schallt, O Taler Weit O Hohen, Jetzt Kommen Die Lustigen Tage, Morgen Will Mein Schatz Abreisen, Ein Heller Und Ein Batzen, Es Blies Ein Jager Wohl In Sein Horn, Was Gleicht Wohl Auf Erden, Im Wald Und Auf Der Heide, Im Krug Zum Grunen Kranze, Trinklied, Fieut Euch Des Lebens, Abschied, Liebchen Ade.
Kommt Ein Vogel Geflogen, Fuchs Du Hast Die Gans Gestohlens, Ich Bin Ein Musikante, Heimliche Liebe, Ich Habe Den Fruhling Gesehen, Vetter Michel, Och Mod'r Ich Well En Ding Han, Fritze Bollmann, Eine Seefahrt Die Ist Lustig, Schiffsjungen Tanz, Wat Wi Doht, Ade Zur Guten Nacht, Guten Abend Gut' Nacht, So Wunsch Ich Ihr Ein Gute Nacht.

FROM EAST TO WEST – A 2 LP cassette
Boil Them Cabbage Down, Bublitschki, Dixie, Don't Be Sad, The Handsome Street Peddlar, *Hornpipe Medley*: Amazon – Jinfikisha – Loro Moira's, Kamarinskaya: The Little Bell, The Lonely Shepherd, *Medley*: Gopak – The Little Apple, *Medley*: Katjuscha – Krakowiak, *Medley*: The Flying Troika – The Lonely Silence Behind The Walls, *Medley*: Gary Owen – Irish Washerwoman – Paddy Whack, *Medley*: Fire On The Mountain – Lary O'Gaff – Shenandoah, *Medley*: Chicken Reel – Turkey In The Straw, Nadjenka, Oh Susanna, Orange Blossom Special, Rhinestone Cowboy, Samara, The beautiful City, Soldier's Joy, Sunshine On The Mountain, Trepak.

GAMES THAT LOVERS PLAY
Games That Lovers Play, A Man And A Woman, Make This Night Last Forever, Never On Sunday, Fly Me To The Moon, This Is My Song.
Lara's Theme, Now I Know, What Now My Love, Elizabeth-Serenade, I Left My Heart In San Francisco.

JAMES LAST GOES POP (U.K.)
For details, see Non Stop Dancing 67/2.

JAMES LAST GOES POP 1 (Holland)
For details, see Non Stop Dancing 66.

JAMES LAST GOES POP 2 (Holland)
For details, see Non Stop Dancing 66/2.

GOLDEN MEMORIES
All Hands On Deck, Goodnight Ladies, Petticoats Of Portugal, From Porto To Barcelona, Lady Of Spain, Toreador's March, Shenandoah, Torna A Surriento, Santa Lucia, Ferry Boat Serenade, Piraus, Never On Sunday, High Barbaree, Hava Nagilah.
If You Knew Susie, Linger Awhile, Elizabeth, Sonny Boy, Just A Gigolo, Valencia, Vier Worte Mocht Ich Dir Jetzt Sagen, Don't Say Goodbye, Komm In Den Park Von Sanssouci, Charleston, Black Bottom, Dream Of The South Seas, Goodnight Sweetheart.

GOLDEN NON STOP DANCING
For details, see Non Stop Dancing 10.

GOODTIMES
For details, see Happyning.

GUITAR A GOGO
12th Street Rag, Jezebel, Espana, Tiritomba, Brazil, La Playa, Fandango.
Funiculi-Funicula, Johnny Guitar, Little Brown Jug, The Breeze And I, Amapola, Who Are We, Vive L'Amour.

HAIR
Aquarius, Frank Mills, Coloured Spade, Ain't Got No, Good Morning Sunshine, Hare Krishna.
Let The Sunshine In, Walking In Space, Easy To Be Hard, Where Do I Go, Hair.

HAMMOND A GOGO
Hello Dolly, Milord, C'est Magnifique, In A Little Spanish Town, Benita, Wheels, Sole Sole Sole, Ich Moch't So Gern Mit Dir Nach Hause Geh'n, Goody Goody, True Love, Moon River, Letkiss, Norskejenka.
America, If I Had A Hammer, Lucky Lips, Du Du Du, Blue Moon, Makin' Whoopee, Cavaquinho, Cumana, Sambarita, Melancholy, La Mamma, Red Roses For A Blue Lady, Bye Bye Blackbird, Auf Wiederseh'n Bei Dir.

HAMMOND A GOGO 2
On The Street Where You Live, I Love Paris, Bye Bye Blues, Patricia, Sweet And Gentle, Managua Nicaragua, Lights Out, Vier Worte Moecht Ich Dir Jetzt Sagen, You Are My Sunshine, Are You Lonesome Tonight, The Candlelight Waltz, Skokiaan, Stars In Your Eyes, Das Leben Ist Wunderbar.
Singin' In The Rain, Bell Bottom Trousers, Deep In The Heart Of Texas, Estrelita, Petticoats Of Portugal, You're Driving Me Crazy, Boo Hoo, Sweet Georgia Brown, Danke Schoen, No Can Do, Samba Estrella, Baiao Cacula, The Peanut Vendor, La Bostella.

HAMMOND A GOGO 3
Volare, You Do Something To Me, Calcutta, Dance Ballerina Dance, Strawberry Cha Cha, If I Were A Rich Man, I Could Have Danced All Night, When You're Smiling, Isabell, The Impossible Dream, Autumn, Salome, Sweet Sue Just You, The Way You Look Tonight.
Tequilla, Papa Loves Mambo, Oh Lonesome Me, It Had To Be You, Roses Of Picardy, Half As Much, The Wedding Samba, El Cumbanchero, La Pachanga, September Song, Serenata, Mame, 'Swonderful, Cherokee.

HAPPY CHRISTMAS FROM JAMES LAST
For details, see Christmas Dancing.

HAPPY HAMMOND
Matilda Matilda, Hi-Lilo Hi-Lo, Music Music Music, Brazilian Love Song, Maruzzella, Lovely Friday, You Do Something To Me, Three Little Words, I Want To Be Happy, Manha De Carnaval, Yellow Bird, Tampico, Moonlight And Roses, Song Of India.
Sucu Sucu, Say Si Si, Minnie From Trinidad.
It Had To Be You, Sweet Caroline, Green Dungarees, Sweet Georgia Brown, You Are My Lucky Star, Who's Sorry Now, The Touch Of Your Lips, Part Of Me, Vieni Vieni, Cachita, Un Poco Rio.

HAPPY LEHAR
This Is The Life For Me, I'm Off To Chez Maxim, Women Women, Vilia, You Are My Hearts Delight, Nobody Loves You As Much As I Do, Beautiful World, On My Lips Every Kiss Is Like Wine, I Love You You Love Me, Laughing Women Are Beautiful, On The Paiho, Song Of The Volga, Silent Lips, My Fair Maiden.
Smiling Happiness Of Mine, Nechledil, The Heavens Blue I'll Get For You, In My Nest Of Heavenly Blue, I Love To Kiss Women, Now The Clouds Have Rolled Away, Stay With Me Forever, Oh Maiden My Maiden, Patiently Smiling, Love What Has Given You This Magic Power, You Alone, He Will Come, Napolitana, Zorika Come Back.

HAPPY MARCHING
Unter Dem Doppeladler, Wien Bleibt Wien, Frei Weg, Gruss An Kiel, Alter Jagermarsch, Mussinan Marsch.
Radetzky Marsch, Blaze Away, Der Petersburger, Karntner Lieder Marsch, Fehrbelliner Reitermarsch, Yorckscher Marsch.

HAPPY MEMORIES
For details, see Wenn Die Elizabeth.

HAPPYNING
Montego Bay, My Sweet Lord, I Hear You Knocking, Neanderthal Man, Girl Of The North Country, Dirty Town.
When I'm Dead And Gone, She Came In Through The Bathroom Window, Cotton Fields, Knock Three Times, Ape Man, The Party Is Over.

HAPPY SUMMER NIGHT
Jealousy, Light Up And Be Happy, The House Of The Rising Sun, Save Me, Photographs.
Secret Love, Granada, Happy Summer Night, Summer Of 42, Dolannes Melody.

JAMES LAST HIS MUSICAL WORLD
Track titles not known.

HUMBA HUMBA A GOGO
Trink Bruderlein Trink, Du Du Liegst Mir Im Herzen, Jetzt Trink'n Ma Noch A Flascheri Wien, Heut' Komm'n Die Engerl'n Auf Urlaub Nach Wien, Kleine Madchen Mussen Schlafen Geh'n, Muss I Denn,

Schutt Die Sorgen In Ein Glaschen Wein, I Had Die Schonen Maderl'n Net Erfunden, O Du Wunderschoner.
Deutscher Rhein, Ich Hab Mein Herz In Heidelberg Verloren, Der Treue Husar, Bummel Petrus, Immer An Der Wand Lang, Oh Susanna.
Lustig Ist Das Zigeunerleben, Rheinische Lieder Schone Frau'n Beim Wein, Oh Wie Bist Du Schon, Waidmannsheil, Fehrbelliner Reitermarsch, Mainzer Narrhalla Marsch, Waldeslust, Du Kannst Nicht Treu Sein, In Munchen Steht Ein Hofbrauhaus, Kornblumen-blau, Wer Soll Das Bezahlen, Humba Humba Tatara, Im Tiefen Keller, So Ein Tag.

IN CONCERT (U.K. GER)
Prelude From L'Arlesienne Suite No. 1, Moonlight Sonata, Ritual Fire Dance, Fur Elise, Pastorale From L'Arlesienne Suite No. 2, Farandole From L'Ariesienne Suite No. 2.
Italian Caprice, Tristesse, Rondo Alla Turca Toccata And Fugue In D Minor.

IN CONCERT (Holland)
For details, see Classics Up To Date 2.

IN CONCERT 2 (Holland)
For details, see In Concert (Ger & U.K.)

IN CONCERT 2 (U.K.)
For details, see Classics.
IN CONCERT 3 (Holland)
For details, see Classics.
IN CONCERT 4 (Holland)
For details, see Classics Up To Date.
IN CONCERT 5 (Holland)
For details, see Classics Up To Date 3.
IN CONCERT 6 (Holland)
For details, see Classics Up To Date 4, but this album does not include Pavane.
IN RUSSIA
Midnight In Moscow, Kalinka, The Red Sarafan, Russian Folk Dance, Cossack Patrol, Lara's Theme.
Sabre Dance, Evening Bells, Two Guitars, Not The Wind, Stenka Rasin, Between Day And Night.
IN SCANDINAVIA
Julia Julia, Gubben Noak, En Jaeger Gik At Jage, Ola Ola Min Eigen Unge, Eg Ser Deg Ut For Gluggien, Marken Er Mejet, Har I Laest Den Berlingske Avis, Taratabomtrala, En Gang I Bredd Med Mig, Kristallen Den Fina, Gladdens Blomster, Teddy Bjornen Fredriksson, Har Kommer Pippi Langstrump, Jag Har Bott Vid En Landsvag.
Gardebylaten, Maggidudi Og Jeg, Kristina Fran Vihelmina, Ack Varmeland Du Skona, Fjariln Vingag Syns Pa Haga, Ljuva Sextital, Pal Sine Honer, Sonnavind Valsen, Lille Sommerfugl, Der Er Lys Lygten.
2371 113 Scandinavia.
IN SOUTH AMERICA
Happy Brasilia, La Bamba, La Paloma, Tico Tico, Malaguena, Tequila, Papa Loves Mambo, Oh Lonesome Me.
Brazil, Perfidia, Guantanamera, Manha De Carnival, Ole O'Cangaceiro, The Wedding Samba, El Combanchero, La Pachanga.
INSTRUMENTALS FOREVER
Moon River, Telstar, Canadian Sunset, Patricia Moonglow & Picnic, Anna.
Theme From A Summer Place, The In Crowd, April In Portugal, Song From The Moulin Rouge, Sail Along Silvery Moon, Delicado.
IN THE MOOD FOR TRUMPETS
In The Mood, Tuxedo Junction, A String Of Pearls, I Know Why, Chattanooga Choo Choo, Moonlight Serenade.
The Volga Boatman, Fools Rush In, That Old Black Magic, St. Louis Blues March, Little Brown Jug, American Patrol.
IN VIENNA
For details, see In Wien Beim Wein.
IN WIEN BEIM WEIN
Es Wird A Wein Sein, Wien Wien Nur Du Allein, Mei Muattarl War A Weanerin, Drunt In Der Lobau, Altes Wiener Fiakerlied, Heut' kommen d'Engerln Auf Urlaub Nach Wien, Wenn Der Herrgott Net Will.
Wiener Pratdrleben, Im Prater Bluhn Wieder Die Baume, Tritsch Tratsch Polka, Ich Sitze Am Kamin, Pizzicato Polka, Jetzt Trink'n Ma Noch A Flascherl Wein.
KAPT'N JAMES BITTET ZUM TANZ
For details, see All Aboard With Cap'n James.
KAPTN JAMES BITTET ZUM TANZ 2
Das Schmeisst Doch Einen Seemann Nicht Gleich Um, Jan Hinnerk, O Signorina Rina Rina, Frisch Auf Alle Mann An Deck, Seerauberlied, Hamburg Ist Ein Schones Stadtchen, Soviel Wind Unk Keine Segel, In Hamburg Liegt Ein Segelschiff Im Hafen, Move Du Fliegst In Die Heimat, Bound To The Ria Grande, Sailing Sailing, Glori Glori Gloria, Wat Wi Dot, Hummel Hummel.
Tabak Und Rum, Schon Ist Die Liebe Im Hafen, Windstarke 12, Abschied Von Der See, Die Reise Nach Jutland, An De Eck Von De Steenstroot, Un Denn Segelt Wi So Langsam Rund Kap Horn, Englischer Schiffsjungentanz, Afscheed, Santa Lucia, Seemann Deine Heimat Ist Das Meer, Ein Schiffein Sah Ich Fahren, Auch Matrosen Haben Eine Heimat, Nun Ade Du Mein Lieb Heimatland.
KAPT'N JAMES AUF ALLEN MEEREN
For details, see Captain James At Seven Seas.
LA MALAGUENA
Mambo No. 5, Cherry Pink And Apple Blossom White, Brazil, Perfidia, Valencia, Delicado, La Malaguena.

Cachita, La Bamba, The Lonely Bull, La Paloma, Tico Tico, Granada, Mexican Hat Dance.
LAS MEJORES ORQUESTAS DEL MUNDO 7
Hello Dolly, Milord, C'est Magnifique, Un Hombre Y Una Mujer, Et Maintenant, Begin The Beguine, Mack The Knife, Anna.
A Summer Place, Il Mundo, Melancolia, La Mamma, April En Portugal, Havah Nagilah.
LAST FOR THE ROAD
Midnight In Moscow, The Air That I Breathe, Romance In F, Wedding Song, MacArthur Park.
Theme From A Summer Place, Moon River, Theme From Elvira Madigan, Cherry Pink And Apple Blossom White, Face In A Crowd, A Man And A Woman, You Make Me Feel Brand New.

LAST OF OLD ENGLAND
The Lass Of Richmond Hill, Rule Britannia, Blow Blow Thou Winter Wind, Begone Dull Care, Polly Oliver, The Banks Of Allen Water, Burton Ale, Where The Bee Sucks, Down Amongst The Bank Of Roses, Early One Morning, The Vicar Of Bray, Simon The Cellarer, Come Lasses And Lads.
The Girl I Left Behind Me, Hearts Of Oak, The British Grenadier, The Farmers Boy, The Miller Of Dee, Drink To Me Only, Widdecombe Fair, Under The Greenwood Tree, With Jockey To The Fair, Roast Beef Of Old England, It Was A Lover And His Lass, Phyllida And Corydon, Cherry Ripe.
LAST THE WHOLE NIGHT LONG – On 2 records/2 LP cassette
All By Myself, Amazing Grace, Belfast, Black Is Black, Boogie, Oogie, Oogie, Brown Girl In The Ring, Cecilia, Daddy Cool, Dancing In The City, Dancing Queen, Devil Woman, Fernando, I Can't Give You Anything, I Love To Love, I Only Want To Be With You, I Write The Songs, If I Only Had time, I'm On Fire, In Zaire, It's A Heartache, I've Got To Get A Message To You, Jeans On, Kiss You All Over, Knowing Me Knowing You, Lara's Theme, Let Me Be The One, Love Hurts, Love Is In The Air, Massachusetts, Money, Money, Money, Mull Of Kintyre, Night Fever, One For You, One For Me, Una Paloma Blanca, Rasputin, Rivers Of Babylon, Rock Bottom, Sailing, Save Your Kisses For Me, Stayin' Alive, Strangers In The Night, Stuff Like That, Substitute, Summertime, Y Viva España, Yes Sir, I Can Boogie, Yesterday, You Make Me Feel Brand New, You're The First, My Last, My Everything, You're The One That I Want.
LES PLUS GRANDS ORCHESTRA
Games That Lovers Play, The In Crowd, Happy Heart, Aquarius, Lara's Theme, American Patrol, That's Life, Toreadors March, Guantanamera, Happy Music, I Left My Heart In San Francisco, The Last Waltz.

JAMES LAST LIVE double album
Opening Music, Evie, Easy Livin', I Left My Heart In San Francisco, Face In A Crowd, Swing Low Sweet Chariot.
Too Fat Polka, Wedding Song, Romance In F Major, Theme From Shaft, I Don't Know How To Love Him.
Also Sprach Zarathustra, Midnight In Moscow, Cossack Patrol, Sabre Dance, Introducing The Band, Vienna Praterleben.
Live And Let Die, Greensleeves, MacArthur Park, Get Back, Ob La Di Ob La Da, La Felicidad.

LIVE IN LONDON (Germany)
Intro 78, Tiger Feet, Radar Love, Jesus Loves You, Bridge Over Troubled Water, Rum And Coca Cola, Quando Quando, South America Take It Away, Cantar Amigos, Schwarze Estrella, Costa Brava, Eso Es El Amor.
Star Wars Theme, West Side Story, Chicken Reel, Turkey In The Straw, Orange Blossom Special, Memories Of Old England, Yes Sir I Can Boogie, Sorry I'm A Lady, Don't Leave Me This Way, Games That Lovers Play.

LIVE IN LONDON double album (U.K.)
Intro 78, Tiger Feet, Radar Love, Jesus Loves You, Bridge Over Troubled Water, I've Got You Under My Skin, Was Ich Dir Sagen Will.
Jog Din Oas, Rum And Coca Cola, Quando Quando Quando, South America Take It Away, The Lonely Shepherd, Larry O Gaff, Fire On The Mountain, Cantar Amigos, Schwarze Estrella, Costa Brava, Eso Es Al Amor.
Theme From Star Wars, West Side Story, With One More Look At You/Watch Closely Now, Love Me Tender, Rip It Up, Don't Be Cruel, Jailhouse Rock, Hound Dog.
Chicken Reel, Turkey In The Straw, Orange Blossom Special, Cockles And Mussels, Daisy Daisy, Abide With Me, Yes Sir I Can Boogie, Sorry I'm A Lady, Don't Leave Me This Way, Don't Cry For Me Argentina, Games That Lovers Play.

THE LOVE ALBUM
Theme From Love Story, Games That Lovers Play, This Is My Song, Lara's Theme, What Now My Love, Guantanamera.
Aquarius, Mr. Tambourine Man, Elizabethan Serenade, You've Lost That Lovin Feeling, I Got You Babe.

LOVE MUST BE THE REASON
Wedding Song, It's Going To Take Some Time This Time, Love Theme From The Godfather, Close To You, The Summer Knows, Heart Of Gold.
Without You, Face In A Crowd, The Way Of Love, I Don't Know How To Love Him, Love Must Be The Reason.

LOVE THIS IS MY SONG
For details, see Games That Lovers Play.

Make the party Last
25 all-time party greats
with james last

MAKE THE PARTY LAST
Cracklin' Rosie, Rose Garden, Knock Three Times, Banks Of The Ohio, Song Sung Blue, Tie A Yellow Ribbon, The Summer Knows, Close To You, Soley Soley, Amarillo, You Are The Sunshine Of My Life, Never Can Say Goodbye.
La Bamba, Hava Nagilha, The Pushbike Song, What Have They Done To Our Song Ma, Joy To The World, What Now My Love, I Don't Know How To Love Him, The Summertime, Goodbye Sam Hello Samantha, I Hear You Knocking, Rock Around The Clock, See You Later Alligator, Hound Dog.

JAMES LAST MEETS HANS LAST (Japan)
Titles not known.

MEIN LEBEN IST MUSIK
Traumerei, In The Mood, Kosaken Patrouille, Dolannes Melody, Freut Euch Des Lebens, Wie Lieblich Schallt, O Taler Weit O Hohen. Sportpalast Polka, Ich Hab'ne Frau, Komm Unter Meine Decke, Du Kannst Nicht Immer Siebzehn Sein, Fernando, Rocky, Lady Love, Wien Bleibt Wien, De Kapt'n De Stuermann De Bootsmann Un Ick, When Irish Eyes Are Smiling.

MELODIE RUSSE (Italy)
For details, see Memories Of Russia.

MEMORIES OF RUSSIA
Don't Be Sad, The Handsome Street Peddlar, Nadjenka, The Little Apple/Gapak, Samara The Beautiful City, Katjuscha/Krakowiak. The Lonely Shepherd, Trepak, Bublitschki, The Flying Troika/The Lonely Silence, The Little Bell, Kamarinskaya.

MIDNIGHT IN DECEMBER
For details, see Christmas Dancing.

MOR
For details, see Beach Party 4.

MR. PARTYKING
American Patrol, I Got You Babe, Delicado, Torreador March, April In Portugal.
Greensleeves, Yesterday, Sail Along Silvery Moon, Adagio From Violin Concerto, La Bamba.

MUSICAL GENIUS OF JAMES LAST
Aquarius, Yesterday, The Lonely Bull, Love Story, Donkey Serenade, El Condor Pasa, Theme From A Summer Place, Mexican Hat Dance.
Games That Lovers Play, American Patrol, Lara's Theme, A Man And A Woman, Elizabethan Serenade, Greensleeves, The Last Waltz, Hava Nagilah.

MUSIC FOR DREAMING
For details, see Classics Up To Date 4.

MUSIC FROM ACROSS THE WAY (USA)
For details, see Beach Party 2 (U.K. version).

MUSIC FROM ACROSS THE WAY (Canada)
Music From Across The Way, Endless Journey, Jerusalem, Wedding Bell Blues, Morning At Seven, Like A Rolling Stone.

Lay Lady Lay, Teenage Love, Distant Woman, At The Height Of The Moon, For Somebody, Baby Don't Go.

MUSIC IS MY LIFE
For details, see Mein Leben Ist Musik.

THE MUSIC OF JAMES LAST double album
In A Persian Market, Adagio From New World Symphony, Polovtsian Dances From Prince Igor, Presto From Symphony No. 7, Moonlight Sonata, Rondo Alla Turca.
Wedding Samba, El Cumbanchero, La Pachanga, The Lass Of Richmond Hill, Rule Britannia, Blow Blow Thou Winter Wind, Begone Dull Care, Villa, You Are My Hearts Delight, Nobody Loves You As Much As I Do, Trumpet Hop, Anvil Polka.
Left My Heart In San Francisco, Elizabethan Serenade, Once On A Sunday Morning, Jean, Cantiga Por Luciana, Music From Across The Way.
Venus, Sugar Sugar, Jelly Tight, When I'm Dead And Gone, Ape Man, Knock Three Times, My Sweet Lord, Here Comes The Sun, Many Blue.

MY FAVOURITE SONGS
I Can See Clearly Now, Dolannes Melody, Have You Never Been Mellow, Don't Cry For Me Argentina, Only You Can.
Summer Of 42, Best Of My Love, Photographs, The Boxer, MacArthur Park.

NABUCCO CLASSICS UP TO DATE
For details, see Classics Up To Date.

NON STOP AND AGOGO
For details, see Portrait Of James Last.

NON STOP DANCING (USA)
Also Sprach Zarathustra, Silver Machine, Children Of The Revolution, Schools Out, Standing In The Road, Easy Livin', Coming Closer, Popcorn, Run To Me, The Guitar Man, Mama Were All Crazee Now, Long Cool Woman In A Black Dress, Pop That Thang, Nothing. Blockbuster, Get Down, Heart Of Stone, Sylvia's Mother, Join Together, Theme From Shaft, Thunder & Lightning, Goodbye To Love, Baby Don't Get Hooked On Me, Tie A Yellow Ribbon, Daniel, Power To All Our Friends, Rock Me Baby, Mini Rock.

NON STOP DANCING 65
Don't Ha Ha, Shake Hands, Can't Buy Me Love, Skinny Minnie, Do Wah Diddy Diddy, Clap Hands, Pretty Woman, Das Ist Die Frage Aller Fragen, Eight Days A Week, Kiddy Kiddy Kiss Me, Good Bye Good Bye Good Bye, My Boy Lollipop, Zwei Madchen Aus Germany, Tennessee Waltz.
Memphis Tennessee, A Hard Days Night, I Feel Fine, No Reply, Kiss And Shake, Downtown, Cincerella Baby, Wer Kann Das Schon, Das War Mein Schonster Tanz, Rag Doll, Melancholie, I Want To Hold Your Hand, Sie Liebt Dich, I Should Have Known Better.

NON STOP DANCING 66
Rock And Roll Music, Vive L'Amour, Not The Lovin Kind, Eve Of Destruction, Like A Rolling Stone, Cadillac, Hang On Sloopy, Marmor Stein Und Eisen, Balla Balla, You've Got Your Troubles, Die Weit Ist So Schon Wie Ein Traum.
Mr. Tambourine Man, Shame And Scandal In The Family, Jack The Ripper.
Help, La La La, Life, Satisfaction, Wooly Bully, Ju Ju Hand, Yesterday, Du Bist Nicht Allein, Baby Don't Go, Siebzehn Jahr Blondes Haar, Love And Kisses, Yookomo, Bag Hand, Hello Josephine.

NON STOP DANCING 66/2
Paint It Black, Paperback Writer, Hello Taxi, The Sun Aint Gonna Shine, Summer In The City, Pretty Flamingo, Red Rubber Ball, Beisz Nicht Gleich In Jeden Apfel, A Man, Strangers In The Night, Yours, Pied Piper, Lil' Red Riding Hood, Hi Lilo Hi Lo.
These Boots Are Made For Walkin, Sure Gonna Miss Her, Get Away, John B, A Lovers Concerto, Yellow Submarine, Eleanor Rigby, Irgend Jemand Liebt Auch Dich, Yesterday Man, Bis Morgen, With A Girl Like You, Hundert Jahre Und Noch Viel Mehr, Blue Beat Girl, Mothers Little Helper.

NON STOP DANCING 67
I'm A Believer, Good Vibrations, Have A Drink On Me, Dear Mrs. Applebee, Super Girl, Das Girl Mit Dem La La La, Spanish Eyes, Green Green Grass Of Home, Friday On My Mind, Stop Stop Stop, It's Last Time, Bend It, Little Man, Save Me.
I Can't Control Myself, No Milk Today, Augen Wie Zwei Sterne, Sugar Town, Mellow Yellow, Black Is Black, Games That Lovers Play,

Good Night My Love, Dandy, Lemon Tree, Happy Jack, Winchester Cathedral, Music To Watch Girls By, Lass Den Dunmen Kimmer.

NON STOP DANCING 67/2
Pleasant Valley Sunday, Death Of A Clown, Farmers Market, Somethin' Stupid, Meine Liebe Zu Dir, I Was Kaiser Bills Batman, Carrie Ann, Windy, Little Bit O' Soul, A Whiter Shade Of Pale, The World We Knew, Baby Come Back, Heroes And Villains, Paper Sun. All You Need Is Love, She'd Rather Be With Me, Okay, Here Comes My Baby, Alternate Title, Mister Pleasant, San Francisco, Silence Is Golden, Ha Ha Said The Clown.
Jackson, Lingering On, Puppet On A String, Una Festa Sui Prati, Komm Allein.

NON STOP DANCING 68
Judy In Disguise, Nobody But Me, Oh Baby Shake, Boogaloo Down Broadway, Bend Me Shape Me, A Banda, Massachusetts, Hello Goodbye, Pata Pata, Daydream Believer, Everlasting Love, Jagerlatein, Eine Schaflose Nacht, Gloryland.
Ballad Of Bonnie & Clyde, Everybody Knows, Gimme Little Sign, Thank You Very Much, Mighty Quinn, John Browns Body, Words, I'm Coming Home, Darlin', Neon Rainbow, Zabadak, Delilah, Poochy, Der Graf Von Luxemburg.

NON STOP DANCING 68/2 (No. 7)
Help Yourself, Mrs. Robinson, It's Time To Go, Simon Says, Mony Mony, Yummy Yummy Yummy, I've Gotta Get A Message To You, Hey Jude, Last Night In Soho, The Son Of Hickory Hollers Tramp, La Felicidad, Master Jack, Gold Auf Der Strasse, Arriverderci Hans.
Jumping Jack Flash, Harper Valley PTA, Sunshine Girl, My Name Is Jack, Days, Do It Again, Fire, Lazy Sunday, If I Only Had Time, A Man Without Love, Young Girl, Moscow, Merci.

NON STOP DANCING 69 (No. 8)
Ob La Di Ob La Da, Chewy Chewy, Eloise, Little Arrows, Those Were The Days, Du Musst Mit Den Wimpern Klimpern, Sweet Inspiration, Boomerang, Touch Me, I Started A Joke, A Minute Of Your Time, Softly Softly, Build Me Up Buttercup, Oh Baby Come Home.
My Little Lady, And Now Here It Comes Again, Lily The Pink, Only One Woman, With A Little Help From My Friends, Good Time Music, Die Liebe Im Allgemeinen, Albatross, Crimson And Clover, Somethings Happening, Love Child, Fox On The Run, Blackberry Way, Azzurro.** **Azzurro missing from U.K. release.

NON STOP DANCING 69/2 (No. 9)
Ballad Of John & Yoko, Green River, Countdown, Lieber Heute Gekusst, Er Steht Im Tor, Nacke Di Nacke Du, Honky Tonk Women, Proud Mary, Oh Happy Day, In The Ghetto, Don't Forget To Remember, Aquarius, Let The Sunshine In, Hare Krishna.
Twenty Five Miles, In The Year 2525, Dynamite Women, Bad Moon Rising, Always Tuesday, Give Peace A Chance, Saved By The Bell, Je T'Aime Moi Non Plus, Love Me Tonight, Heute So Morgen So, Star Parade, Dizzy, Everyday People, Mendocino.

NON STOP DANCING 70 (No. 10)
Na Na Hey Hey Kiss Him Goodbye, In A Gadda Da Vida, Oh Well,

Anuschka, Abendstunde Hat Gold Im Munde, Geh Alte, Schau Mi Net So Teppert An, Venus, Sugar Sugar, Jam Up And Jelly Tight, He Aint Heavy He's My Brother, The Windmills Of Your Mind, Jingle Jangle, Number One, Down On The Corner.

Heya, Tonight Today, Deep Water, John Lee Hooker Tracy, Gruezi Wohl Frau Stirnima, One Million Years, Sunshine Of Your Love, Come Together, Take A Letter Maria, All Together Now, Raindrops Keep Fallin On My Head, Mighty Joe, Suspicious Minds.

NON STOP DANCING 71 (No. 11)

Up Around The Bend, Yellow River, Soolaimon, Ra Ta Ta, Er Hat Ein Knallrotes, Ringel Dingel Klingelding, Spill The Wine, All Right Now, A Song Of Joy, The Wonder Of You, Greensleeves, Cecilia, Black Night, Lookin Out My Back Door, Questions, Groovin With Mr. Bloe, Are You Ready, Lola, El Condor Pasa, Neanderthal Man, Jerusalem.

Candida, In The Summertime, Goodbye Sam Hello Samantha, Superman, American Woman, Love Like A Man, Natural Sinner.

NON STOP DANCING 12

Hey Tonight, She's A Lady, What Is Life, Cracklin Rosie, Rose Garden, Ich Bin Verliebt In Die Liebe, No Matter What, Silver Moon, After Midnight, Amazing Grace, Love Story, But I Can Sleep In A Park, San Bernadino, The Man From Nazareth.

Be My Baby, Immigrant Song, Stranger Kind Of Woman, The Pushbike Song, What Have They Done To My Song Ma, Oh Wann Kommst Du, Another Day, Have You Ever Seen The Rain, Manja, Ruby Tuesday, Sunshine, Ape Man, Knock Three Times, My Sweet Lord.

NON STOP DANCING 72 (No. 13)

Intro, Co Co, Saah Saah Kumba Kumba, Never Ending Song Of Love, Zeig Mir Den Platz An Der Sonne, Butterfly, Get It On, What Are You Doin' Sunday, Let Your Yeah Be Yeah, Rainy Days And Mondays, Che Sara, Sweet Hitch Hiker, Put Your Hand In The Hand, One Day.

Hey Willy, Tap Turns On The Water, Ten Bananas, Pour Un Flirt, Tonight, Uncle Albert/Admiral Halsey, He's Gonna Step On You Again, Tweedle Dee Tweedle Dum, Spanish Harlem, Music From Across The Way, Ich Zeig Dir Den Sonnenschein, Loop Di Love, Hello Buddy, Vive L'Amour.

NON STOP DANCING 72/2

Fireball, Beautiful Sunday, Samson And Delilah, Am Tag Als Conny Kramer Starb, How Do You Do, Soley Soley, Amarillo, Never Before, Heart Of Gold, Apres Toil, Sacramento, Telegram Sam, Son Of My Father, Schone Maid.

Back Off Boogaloo, Mexican Puppeteer, Ring A Ring Of Roses, Tumbling Dice, One Way Wind, Santanando, Poppa Joe, Without You, I Will Return, I'd Like To Teach The World To Sing, Beg Steal Or Borrow, Komm Gib Mir Deine Hand, Lady Sue, Cotton Fields.

NON STOP DANCING 73 (No. 14)

Silver Machine, Children Of The Revolution, Schools Out, Hello A, Black And White, Standing In The Road, Easy Livin, Coming Closer, Popcorn, Run To Me, The Guitar Man, I'm On My Way, Michaela, Viva Espana.

Mama Weer All Crazee Now, Long Cool Woman In A Black Dress, Pop That Thang, Sylvias Mother, Join Together, Bottoms Up, Nothing, Theme From Shaft, Thunder And Lightning, Goodbye To Love, Baby Don't Get Hooked On Me, Wig Wam Bam, Lets Dance, Rock and Roll Pt. 2.

NON STOP DANCING 73/2 (No. 15)

Also Sprach Zarathustra, Rock Me Baby, Mini Rock, Tie A Yellow Ribbon, Immer Wieder Sonntags, Mama Loo, Wenn Ein Schiff Voruberfahrt, Dreams Are Ten A Penny, It Never Rains In Southern California, Yellow Boomerang, Crazy Horses, Daniel, Ein Festival Der Liebe, Cum On Feel The Noize.

Block Buster, Get Down, Heart Of Stone, Power To All Our Friends, By The Devil, Cover Of The Rolling Stone, Knock Out, Woman From Tokyo, Hi Hi Hi, Me And Mrs. Jones, Never Never Never, Proud Mary, Get Back.

NON STOP DANCING 74 (No. 16)

You Want To Dance, I'm The Leader Of The Gang, Saturday Nights Alright For Fighting, Say Has Anybody Seen My Sweet Gypsy Rose, Top Of The World, Alright Alright Alright, Goodbye Yellow Brick Road, Angie, 48 Crash, Skweeze Me Pleeze Me, Can The Can, Feeling Stronger Everyday, Heart Beats Like A Love Beat, Rubber Bullets.

Ballroom Blitz, My Friend Stan, Photographs, Ooch Baby, Higher Ground, Were An American Band, Touch Me In The Morning, Knocking On Heavens Door, Brother Louie, The Free Electric Band, Half Breed, Joy To The World, Hot Love.

NON STOP DANCING 74/2

Do You Wanna Dance, Who Ever Told You, Devil Gate Drive, Shady Lady, Du Kannst Nicht Immer Siebzehn Sein, Spaniens Gitarren, The Air That I Breathe, Seasons In The Sun, Jet, My Coo Ca Choo, The Loco Motion, TSOP.

This Flight Tonight, Teenage Rampage, Waterloo, Juanita, Hooked On A Feeling, Oh My My, Best Thing That Ever Happened To Me, Living For The City, Tiger Feet, Radar Love, Jesus Loves You, Dan The Banjo Man, Exodus.

NON STOP DANCING 76 (No. 17)

I'm On Fire, Morning Sky, A.I.E. (MWANA), Do It Anyway You Wanna, Foot Stompin Music, Julie Anne, Lady Lay, Du Sag Einfach Du, Sailing, Donallnes Melodie, Rice And Beans, Blow Your Whistle.

Welcome To The Party, That's The Way I Like It, Change With The Times, Lady Bump, Get Down Tonight, What A Difference A Day Makes, Fly Robin Fly, One Of These Nights, The Hustle, I Can't Give You Anything But My Love, Brazil, Polamo Blanca, Funky Inn.

NON STOP DANCING 76/2

You Wanna Dance, Pinball Wizard, 1-2-3-4 Fire, Da Kommt Jose Der Strassenmusikant, The Lies In Your Eyes, Mississippi, Bumpin', Queen Of Clubs, Sing It Out, Motorcycle Mama, Surrender, Love Hurts, Long Train Runnin', Love Machine.

Theme From S.W.A.T., Get Up And Boogie, You Sexy Thing, I Love To Love, Save Your Kisses For Me, Schmidtchen Schleicher, Fernando, Rocky, Lady Love, I Write The Song, All By Myself, See You Later, Hound Dog.

NON STOP DANCING 77 (Number 18)

Run Back To Mama, Don't Go Breaking My Heart, Dancing Queen, Horoscope, Silver Bird, Getaway, Play That Funky Music, Heaven Is In The Backseat Of My Cadillac, Howzat, Dance Little Lady Dance, Beautiful Noise, Monza, I Only Wanna Be With You, School Days.

Disco Duck, Bump De Bump Yo Booty, New York Disco, Devil Woman, Jeans On, More More More, In Zaire, Daddy Cool, Money Money Money, Sweet Love, Feel The Shelter, Dream Weaver, Shake Your Booty.

NON STOP DANCING 77/2 (Number 19)

Under The Moon Of Love, Living Next Door To Alice, Livin' Thing, Da Doo Ron Ron, Africa Man, Blinded By The Light, Love Me, I'm In Love, Night And Day, If You Leave Me Now, Knowing Me Knowing You.

Music Train, Don't Leave Me This Way, Hey Baby, Get It Down, I'm Your Boogie Man, Car Wash, Far Away, Boogie Nights, Tom's Bridge, What Can I Say, Sing A Song, Sunny.

NON STOP DANCING 78 FOLGE 25

Dancing Party, Saturday Night, Daddy Cool, Belfast, Put Your Love In Me, Desiree, Lady In Black, Give A Little Bit, Miss Broadway, House Of The Rising Sun, Mull Of Kintyre.

Dance Dance Dance, Love Is In The Air, Get Off Your Aah And Dance, Liebelei, Needles And Pins, Its A Heartache, Black Is Black, Singin' In The Rain, King Of Discos, Fun, Keep It Comin' Love, Shout It Out Loud.

NON STOP DANCING 20 Jubilaums double album

Jubilation, You Are The Sunshine Of My Life, Never Can Say Goodbye, Doctors Orders, Your The First My Last My Everything, Lady Marmalade, Take A Look Ahead, You Ain't Seen Nothing Yet, The Bridge, Goodbye My Love, Giddy Up Giddy Up A Ding Dong, Please Mr. Postman, Inspiration.

Fancy Pants, Let Me Be The One, Juke Box Jive, Griechischer Wein, Kung Fu Fighting, The Night Chicago Died, Laughter In The Rain, Lu Le La, Pick Up The Pieces, The Bertha Butt Boogie, Express, Sound Your Funky Horn, Shame Shame Shame.

Don't Ha Ha, Shake Hands, Can't Buy Me Love, Skinny Minnie, Do Wah Diddy Diddy, Clap Hands, Pretty Woman, Das Ist Die Frage Aller Fragen, Eight Days A Week, Kiddy Kiddy Kiss Me, Good Bye Good Bye Good Bye, My Boy Lollipop, Zwei Madchen Aus Germany, Tennessee Waltz.

Memphis Tennessee, A Hard Days Night, I Feel Fine, No Reply, Kiss And Shake, Downtown, Cinderella Baby, Wer Kann Das Schon, Dar War Mein Schonster Tanz, Rag Doll, Melancholie, Sie Liebt Dich, I Want To Hold Your Hand, I Should Have Known Better.

NON STOP DANCING 66 double album
For details, see Non Stop Dancing 65 & 66.
NON STOP DANCING 67 double album
For details, see Non Stop Dancing 66/2 & 67.
NON STOP DANCING 68 double album
For details, see Non Stop Dancing 67/2 & 68.
NON STOP DANCING 69 double album
For details, see Non Stop Dancing 7 & 8.
NON STOP DANCING 70 double album
For details, see Non Stop Dancing 9 & 10.
NON STOP DANCING 71 double album
For details, see Non Stop Dancing 11 & 12.
NON STOP DANCING 72 double album
For details, see Non Stop Dancing 72 & 72/2.
NON STOP DANCING 73 double album
For details, see Non Stop Dancing 73 & 73/2.
NON STOP DANCING 74 double album
For details, see Non Stop Dancing 74 & 74/2.
NON STOP DANCING 75 double album
For details, see Non Stop Dancing Vol. 20 & 76.
NON STOP DANCING '81
Can't Stop The Music, Coming Up, Eldorado, Everything Works If
You Let It, Fanfare For The Common Man, Feels Like I'm In Love,
Gimme Some Lovin', Jump To The Beat, Late In The Evening,
Lovely One, Master Blaster, Matador, Red Light, Santa Maria, The
Seduction, Sexy Eyes, Take Your Time, Ten O'clock Postman, They
Do The Samba, Why, Xanadu, You're O.K.
NON STOP DANCING SPECIAL (U.K.)
For details, see Non Stop Dancing 66.
NON STOP DISCO DANCING (Canada)
For details, see Non Stop Dancing 20 from Jubilation to Shame Shame
Shame.
NON STOP DISCO DANCING (Japan)
That's The Way I Like It, Change With The Times, Lady Bump,
TSOP, Me And Mrs. Jones, Living For The City, Higher Ground, Get
Down Tonight, Pick Up The Pieces, The Bertha Butt Boogie,
Express, Sound Your Funky Horn, Shame Shame Shame.
The Hustle, I'm On Fire, Do It Anyway You Wanna, Kung Fu
Fighting, You Are The Sunshine Of My Life, Never Can Say
Goodbye, Doctors Orders, Your The First The Last My Everything,
Lady Marmalade, Take A Look Ahead, Brazil, Fly Robin Fly, Funky
Inn.
NON STOP DISCO DANCING 2 (Canada)
For details, see Non Stop Dancing 17.
NON STOP DISCO DANCING 2 (Japan)
Shake Your Booty, Sing It Out, Disco Duck, Bump De Bump Yo
Booty, New York Disco, More More More, Daddy Cool, Getaway,
Play That Funky Music, Heaven Is In The Backseat Of My Cadillac.
Save Me, Light Up And Be Happy, 1-2-3-4 Fire, Queen Of Clubs,
Theme From S.W.A.T., Get Up And Boogie, You Sexy Thing, You
Wanna Dance, Bumpin', Love Machine.
NON STOP DANCING INTERNATIONAL (Spain)
For details, see Non Stop Dancing 69/2.
NON STOP EVERGREENS
For details, see Evergreens Non Stop Dancing.
OLE
Granada, La Paloma, Cherry Pink And Apple Blossom White,
Patricia, La Bamba, Tico Tico, Brazil, Amapola, Amor, Delicado, The
Bandit, Carmen 68.
ONDER MOEDERS PARAPLU
Drie Maal Drie Is Negen, Eeen Twee Drie Vier, Daar Was Een
Vrouw Die Koeken Bakken Zou, 'k Heb m'n Wagen Volgeladen, Ik
Zag Twee Beren, Berend Botje Gong Oet Voaren, Jan Mijne Man,
Groene Zwanen Witte Zwanen, Ozewiezewoze, Moriaantje Zoo Zwat
Als Roet, Boer Wat Zeg Je Van Mijn Kippen, In Den Haag, Hansje
Pansje Kevertje, Onder Moeders Paraplu.
Twee Violen En Een Bas Bas Bas Bas, Drie Kleine Kleutertjes, Hop
Maar Janneke, Twee Emmertjes Water Halen, Daar Is Een Kindeke
Geboren, Rijen Rijen Rijen In Een Wagentje, Zeg Ken Jij De
Mosselman, De Advocaat, 'k Zou Zoo Graag Een Ketting Breien, Heb
Je Wel Gehoord, Hop Hop Paardje, Ik Stond Laatst Voor Een
Poppenkraam, Ik D'r Van Jaap, Daar Zaten zeven Kikkertjes.
OP KLOMPEN
Hoog Op De Gele Wagen, Een Karretje Op De Zandweg Reed, De

Paden Op De Lanen In, Hela Gij Bloempjes, In't Groene Dal In't
Stille Dal, Langs Berg En Dal Klinkt Hoorngeschal, 't Zonnetje Gaat
Van Ons Scheiden, Moeke D'r Staait'n Vrijer Bie De Deur, Catootje,
Daar Kwam Ene Boer Van Zwitserland, In Holland, Vier Weverkens,
Hoe Zachikens Glijdt Ons Bootje, Knaapje Zag Een Roosje Staan.
Door De Bossen Door De Beide, Limburg Mijn Vaderland, De
Bloempjes Gingen Slapen, Op De Grote Stille Heide, 'n Boer Wol
Noar Zien Noaber Tou, Het Kwezelken, Daar Was Laatst Een Meisje
Loos, Wel Annamarieke, Des Winters Als Het Regent, Wie Rusten
Wil In't Groene Woud, Roodborstje Tikt Tegen Het Raam, De
Wielewaal, De Uil Zat In De Olme, Een Vreemde Arme Snuiter.
JAMES LAST PARTY double album
Morning At Seven, I Got You Babe, My Love, Sail Along Silvery
Moon, Outing, Moonlight Over The Mountain, Delicado, Fly Me To
The Moon, La Bamba, The World Needs Love, Funiculi-Funicula.
Gaylord, Greensleeves, Mack The Knife, America, Lingering On,
Seaside Holiday, Yesterday, Caravan, What Now My Love, Amapola.
PARTY DANCING 1
For details, see Non Stop Dancing 65.
PARTY DANCING 2
For details, see Non Stop Dancing 66.
PARTY SNACKS
Lay Lady Lay, Canadian Sunset, Mr. Tambourine Man, La Bamba,
Down By The Riverside.
Proud Mary, Cecilia, Let The Sunshine In, I Hear You Knocking,
House Of The Rising Sun.
PIANO A GOGO
Java, My Bonnie, Maria, Happy Days Are Here Again, Lingering On,
Mack The Knife, Everybody Loves A Lover.
Love Me Or Leave Me, Bei Mir Bist Du Schon, The House Of The
Rising Sun, America, Mexico City, Poeme, My Guys Come Back.

. . . PLAYS JOHANN STRAUSS
Annen Polka, Eljen A Magyar, Emperor Waltz, Leichtes Blut,
Radetzky March, Roses From The South, Tales From the Vienna
Woods, Thunder And Lightning, Voices Of Spring.
JAMES LAST PLAYS ROBERT STOLZ
Two Hearts In Three Four Time, My Song Of Love, Lovely Vienna
Mine, The Mood For Lovers, Fair Or Dark I Love Them All, You
Shall Be King Of My Heart, Say You Say You To Me, You Too,
Goodbye, Springtime In Vienna, Gipsy Violin.
We Are Young We Are Full Of Life, Charming Weather, Where Is It
Where, Yearning For You, Vienna Where Wine And Waltz Are
Blooming, Your Eyes, Don't Say Goodbye, Come Into The Park Of
Sanssouci, Salome, Before My Fathers House, The Last Rose Is
Blooming.

JAMES LAST PLAYS FOR YOU four record boxed set
Record One: Left My Heart In San Francisco, Mexico City, Malaguena, April In Portugal, Midnight In Moscow, Around The World, Guantanamera, Canadian Sunset, The Pearl Fishers, Havah Nagilah, Moulin Rouge, Sabre Dance.
Record Two: Brazil, Quando Quando, Cherry Pink And Apple Blossom White, Siboney, Fandango, Tequila, El Condor Pasa, A Banda, The Bandit, Java, U Poci Rio, La Paloma.
Record Three: Happy Heart, Mr. Tambourine Man, Fly Me To The Moon, The Party Is Over, Help Me Girl, Time After Time, Love Must Be The Reason, Games That Lovers Play, Passion Flower, A Man And A Woman, Close To You, You've Lost That Lovin Feeling.
Record Four: Song Sung Blue, Jesus Christ, How Do You Do, Amazing Grace, Poppa Joe, Wedding Song, Cecilia, Beautiful Sunday, House Of The Rising Sun, Blowin' In The Wind, Proud Mary, Let The Sunshine In.

POLKA PARTY
Standchen, Trompeten-Muckel, Schutzenliesel, Tritsch-Tratsch Polka, Untern Linden, Liechtensteiner Polka.
She's Too Fat For Me, Die Muhle Im Schwarzwald, Flieger Marsch, Amboss Polka, Annen Polka, Heinzelmannchens Wachparade.

POLKA PARTY 2
Adelheid, Haselnuttspolka, Tiroler Holzhackerbuab'm, Die Spieluhr, Trompeten-Jodler.
Schwarze Amsel, Anneliese, Paris Polka, Die Rose Vom Worthersee, Hofkonzert Im Hinterhaus, Herz Schmerz Polka.

POLKA PARTY 3
Wochenend Und Sonnenschein, Im Kahlenbergerdorfel, Happy Cowboy, Meine Rosa Ist Aus Bohmen, Rusticanella, Sportpalast Polka.
Rosamunde, Siamesische Wachtparade, Schwedenmadel, Lotusblumen, Esels Polka, Polka Francaise.

PORTRAIT OF JAMES LAST
Greensleeves, The Song From The Moulin Rouge, Barcarole, I Got You Babe, Eine Ganze Nacht, Cherry Pink And Apple Blossom White, Sail Along Silvery Moon, Somewhere My Love.
Hello Dolly, Milord, C'est Magnifique, John B, A Lovers Concerto, Yellow Submarine, Estrellita, In Portugal, Mr. Tambourine Man, Shame And Scandel In The Family, Jack The Ripper, Du Du Liegst Mir Im Herzen, Der Mai Ist Im Herzen, Das Wandern Ist Des Mullers Lust. 1236 071 Holland.

JAMES LAST PRESENTS GEORGE WALKER
Who Are We, Theres A Kind Of Hush, Danny Boy, Plaisir D'Amour, Games That Lovers Play, Et Maintenant.
Goin Out Of My Head, Alfie, What Now My Love, Malaguena Salerosa, Please Come Back, If You Go Away.

ROCK AROUND WITH ME
Rock Around The Clock, See You Later Alligator, Hound Dog, Blueberry Hill, Hanky Panky, Mini Rock, Lady Madonna, Rock And Roll Music, Rock Around The World, By The Light Of The Silvery Moon, That's My Desire, Whole Lotta Shakin Goin On, Charlie Brown, When The Saints Go Marching In.
Ready Teddy, Diana, Shake Rattle And Roll, Back To Memphis, Don't Be Cruel, Jailhouse Rock, Isle Of Capri, Buona Sera, Oh Marie, Ramblin Rose, Back In Town, Summertime Blues, Muskrat Ramble, Rip It Up.

ROCK ME GENTLY
Sweet City Woman, Indiana Wants Me, Dun-robins Gone, Sundown, One Fine Morning.
Carry On, Rock Me Gently, If You Could Read My Mind, For Better For Worse, The Night They Drove Old Dixie Down.

ROLLING HOME WITH CAPTAIN JAMES
For details, see All Aboard With Captain James.

ROLLING HOME WITH CAPTAIN JAMES 2
For details, see Kapt'n James Bittet Zum Tanz 2.

ROMANTIC DREAMS
Abide With Me, Amazing Grace, Careless Love, Cockles And Mussels, Country Train, Es Waren Zwei Königskinder, Going Home, The Londonderry Air, Paintings, The Rose Of Tralee, Scarborough Fair, When Irish Eyes Are Smiling, Yosaku.

RUSSIA BETWEEN DAY AND NIGHT
For details, see In Russia.

RUSSLAND ERINNERUNGEN
For details, see Memories Of Russia.

RUSSLAND ZWISCHEN TAG UND NACHT
For details, see In Russia.

SAX A GOGO
Bye Bye Blackbird, Siboney, Il Mondo, The More I See You, Charmaine, What Now My Love, Little Man.
Amor, La Cucaracha, O Sole Mio, You Are My Sunshine, 500 Miles, Clementine, Dandy.

SING MIT
Sing Sing Party Sing, Blau Blau Blau Bluht Der Enzian, Manana, Ich Fang'fur Euch Den Sonnenschein, Mohikana Shalali, Ladi Lau Heut' Gehn Wir Nicht Nach Haus, Rot Ist Der Wein, Jetzt Trink' Ma No A Flascherl Wein Wir Machen Durch Bis Morgen Fruh, Ich Hab' Die Liebe Geseh'n, Babuschkin, Fiesta Mexicana, Jambalaya, Hey Capello.
Tanz Bitte Noch Einmal Mit Mor, Jeder Hat Dic Gern Einer Hat Dich Lieb, Dass Du Much Liebst Das Weiss Ich, Oh Wie Wohl Ist Mir, Geh Zum Teufel Kleiner Engel, Du Bist Viel Zu Schon Um Alleine Nach Hause Zu Geh'n Komm Mit Nach Madeira, Valencia, Eviva Espana, Ich Wunsch Mir Ne Kleine Miezekatze, Und Wenn Dazu Die Musik Spielt, Drei Chinesen, Azzurro, Trizonesien Song.

SING MIT 2
Rucki-Zucki, Jetzt Geht Die Party Richtig Los, Geh' Alte Schau Mi Net So Teppert An, Edelweiss, Junge Die Welt Ist Schon, Sing Mit Sing Mit, Schones Madchen Aus Arcadia, Goodbye Mama, Skandal Im Harem, Auf Der Mauer Auf Der Lauer, Lore Lore Lore, Freu' Dich Doch, John Brown, Jagerlatein.
Prost Skal Salute, Lieber Heute Gekusst, Mein Schatz Du Bist 'Ne Wucht, Dreh Dich Weiter Ballerina, Ich Komm Bald Weider, Liebe Gluck Und Sonnenschein, Hasta La Vista, Die Carmen Sagt Si Si, Tanze Mit Mir In Den Morgen, Wenn Der Schnee Fallt Auf Die Rosen, Wie Damals In Paris, Wir Zwei Fahren Irgenwohin, Bella Italia, Wenn Die Sonne Scheint Denkt Keiner An Den Regen.

SING MIT 3
Ja Mir San Mit'n Randl Da, Meine Oma Fahrt Im Huhnerstall, O Wie Bist Du Schon, Zigeunerwagen, Aber Am Abend Da Spielt Der Zigeuner, Lustig Ist Das Zigeunerleben, Ich Bin Von Kopf Bis Fuss Auf Liebe Eingestellt, Diesen Tango Tanz Ich Nur Mit Dir, Polenmadcher, Gib' Mir Den Wodka Schmadahupfl'n, Ole O Cangaceiro, Zieh' Den Koff Aus Der Schlinge Bruder John.
Hab'Mein Wagen Vollgeladen, Komm Und Sing Mit, Mein Vater War Ein Wandersmann, Marie Der Letzte Tanz Ist Nur Fur Dich, Du Kannst Das Am Besten, Ich Mach' Ein Gluckliches Madchen Aus Dir, Uberall Bluhen Rosen, Du Frangst Den Wind Niemals Ein, Wozu Ist Die Strasse Da, Das Leben Ist Wunderbar, . . . Raus Bist Du, Komm Trink Und Trink, La Felicidad.

SING MIT 4
Wenn Die Rosen Erbluhen In Malaga, Ein Koffer Und Zwei Gitarren, Die Schwarze Barbara, Zehn Kleine Magdelein, Wenn Das So Weitergeht, Simsalabim, Mein Herz Das Ist Ein Bienenhaus, Ich Hab' Noch Sand In Den Schuh'n Aus Hawaii, Der Letzte Sirtaki, Du Sag' Einfach Du, Ole Wir Machen Jagd Auf Den Torero, Ja Ja Der Chiantiwein, Lady Of Spain.
Der Grosse Xampano, Ich Mocht' Auf Einer Insel Leben, Ja Ja Der Peter Der Ist Schlau, Du Gehst Fort, Wart' Auf Mich, Erst Beim Tango Werd' Ich Richtig Munter, Taram Taram Tam-Tam, Wenn Der Toni Mit Der Vroni, Auf Der Alm Da Gibt's Koa Sund', Ich Hab' Ne Frau, Komm Unter Meine, Decke, Du Kannst Nicht Immer Siebzehn Sein, Ri-Ra-Rutz, Bis Fruh' Um Funte.

SING MIT 5
Hier Ist Was Los, Rosa Rosa, Die Lustigen Holzhackerbaum, Der Wein War Aus Bordeaux, Tango D'amour, Der Weisse Flieder, Guck Da Tapst Der Hans Verstohlen, Mein Kafer Fliegt, Ananas, Charly Lass Dir Einen Bart Steh'n, Ich Lass Mir Meinen Korper Schwarz Bepinseln, Egon, Die Madchen Aus Dem Kohlenpott, Maria Helen.
Cheerio, El Paradiso, Tobago Helloh, Ein Mannlein Liegt Im Walde, Wir Klappern Mit Muh' Alle Wir Klappern Mit Muh' alle Wirtshauser Ab, Das War John Nie Passiert, Ein Korn Im Feldbett, Ein Sonntag Im Bett, Sommer In Der Stadt, Marie Ich Komm'zu Dir, Gulliwadka, Rixd orfer, Die Party War Schon, Nach Hause Geh'n Wir Nicht.

SING MIT 6 VON HAMBURG BIS MEXICO
Cantar Amigos, Schwarze Estrella, Costa Brava, Eso Es El Amor, Madalena, Manzanillo, Einmal Nach Sevilla, Gracias Amigos, Meine Maus Die Heisst Klaus, Maria Bonita, Diese Nacht, Espana Cani, Ich

Weiss Was Dirfehit, Tristeza.
Ich Trink'den Wein Nich Gern Allein, Das Gibt's Nur Auf Der Reeperbahn Bei Nacht, Die Nacht Ist Nicht Allein Zum Schlafen Da, Der Onkel Doktor Hat Gesagt, Kannst Du Pfeifen Johanna, Ich Pfeif'heut Nacht Vor Deinem Fenster, Ja Das Haben Die Madchen So Gerne, Ganz Ohne Weiber Geht Die Chose Nicht, Frauen Und Wein, Sieben Fasser Wein, San Diego Train, Heut'mach'ich Hochzeit Mit Marie, Wer Wind Denn Weinen Wenn Man Auseinandergeht, Ein Prosit Der Gemutlichkeit.

SOFT ROCK
Lay Lady Lay, I Got You Babe, Teenage Love, Mr. Tambourine Man, Ballad Of Easy Rider, Yesterday.
Like A Rolling Stone, Wedding Bell Blues, Baby Don't Go, For Somebody, You've Lost That Lovin Feelin'.

SOUND OF JAMES LAST
Winchester Cathedral, Time After Time, Games That Lovers Play, Help Me Girl, Lingering On, That's Life.
Born Free, The Day We Said Goodbye, Go Away Little Girl, My Love, Strolling Through Gateshead, Guantanamera.

SOUTH OF TIJUANA double album
Record One: La Bamba, Cherry Pink And Apple Blossom White, Mexican Hat Dance, Passion Flower, Delicado, Wheels, Never On Sunday, La Paloma, Ava Maria No Morro, Tico Tico.
Record Two: Happy Music, Begin The Beguine, Skokjaan, La Golondrina, Guatanamera, Secret Love, Carmen 68, La Mer, Un Poco Rio, Perfidia.

JAMES LAST SPIELT ROBERT STOLZ
For details, see James Last Plays Robert Stolz.

STAR PORTRAIT double album
Record One: The Battle Of Bilbao, Hora Staccato, Granada, No Words, Sabeltanz, Happy Brasilia, Calypso, Greensleeves, Wenn Suss Das Mondlicht Auf Den Hugeln Schlaft, American Patrol, Jerusalem, Telstar.
Record Two: Love Story, Secret Love, Morgens Um Sieben Ist Die Welt Noch In Ordnung, Memories Of Rubinstein, Mr. Tambourine Man, Happy Music, Lara's Theme, El Condor Pasa, Games That Lovers Play, Ballad Of The Easy Rider, Kalinka, Elvira Madigan.

STARS IM ZEICHEN EINES GUTEN STERNS
James Last	Annie Laurie
	Greensleeves
Lars Berghagen	Aloha Oe
	La Paloma
	Und Dann Ging Ich Zu Den

Abba	Pick A Bale Of Cotton
	On Top Of Old Smokey
	Midnight Special
Bata Illic	Auf Der Strasse Zu Dir
	Katjuschka
	Kalinka
James Last	Danny Boy
	Plaisir D'Amour
	The House Of The Rising Sun
Freddy	Guantanamera
	La Golondrina
	Cielito Lindo
Wencke Myhre	Tiritomba
	Holzschuhtanz
	Tritsch Tratsch Polka
Fischer Chore	Horch Was Kommt Von Draussen
	Jetzt Kommen Die Lustigen
Karel Gott	Swanee River
	When The Saints Go Marching In
James Last	Glory Glory
	Wenn Wir Heut Auseinandergehn

Production James Last.

STEREO SPECTACULAR
She's Too Fat For Me, Love Theme From The Godfather, Se A Cabo, Liechtensteiner Polka, Theme From Love Story, Poppa Joe. Schuetzenliebel, I Am I Said, Tritsch Tratsch Polka, A Man And A Woman, Love Must Be The Reason.

SUCCESS POOR DANSER
Details were not known at time of going to press.

SUPER NON STOP DANCING double album
Don't Ha Ha, Shake Hands, Can't Buy Me Love, No Reply, Kiss And Shake, Downtown, Satisfaction, Wooly Bully, Ju Ju Hand, Yesterday, Du Bist Nicht Allein, Baby Don't Go, 17 Jahr Blondes Haar, Balla Balla.
John B, A Lovers Concerto, Yellow Submarine, Yesterday Man, Bis Morgen, With A Girl Like You, Dandy, Lemon Tree, It's The Last Time, Spanish Eyes, Green Green Grass Of Home, Winchester Cathedral, Music To Watch Girls By, Lass Den Dunmen Kummer.
Ob La Di Ob La Da, Chewy Chewy, Eloise, Love Me Tonight, Heute So Morgen So, Star Parade, I've Gotta Get A Message To You, Hey Jude, Anuschka, Abendstunde Hat Gold Im Munde, Oh Happy Day, Aquarius, Let The Sunshine In, Hare Krishna.
Jumping Jack Flash, Harper Valley PTA, Help Yourself, Mrs. Robinson, It's Time To Go, Simon Says, Mony Mony, Yummy Yummy Yummy, Rock Around The Clock, Charlie Brown, When The Saints Go Marchin' In, Little Arrows, Those Were The Days, Du Musst Mit Den Wimpern Klimpern.

SUPER PARTY PAC
Power To The People, Proud Mary, Little Arrows, Those Were The Days, Sweet Hitch Hiker, Put Your Hand In The Hand, Theme From Shaft, Thunder And Lightning, Daniel, Cracklin Rosie, Rose Garden, Yellow River, Ob La Di Ob La Da, After Midnight, Crazy Horses, The Pushbike Song, Aquarius, Let The Sunshine In, Hey Tonight, She's A Lady, Joy To The World, Chirpy Chirpy Cheep Cheep, Ballad Of John And Yoko, Green River, Easy Livin', Greensleeves, Tie A Yellow Ribbon, American Woman, Long Cool Woman In A Black Dress, Popcorn, Black And White, It Never Rains In Southern California, Knock Three Times, Get Down, Rock 'n Roll Part 2.

SUPER STEREO 74
Proud Mary, Killing Me Softly, Jenny Jenny, Sing A Simple Song, Without You.
Adelheid, Montego Bay, Blowin' In The Wind, Wedding Bell Blues, Mamy Blue.

TAKE IT EASY (Collection)
TANGO
A Media Luz, Adios Muchachos, Adios, Pampa Mia, Amargura, Blue Sky, Blue Tango, Caminito, La Cumparsita, Dancing The Tango, Flutes Tango, Rosita, Tango.

TEN YEARS NON STOP
For details, see Non Stop Dancing 20.

THAT'S LIFE
For details, see The Sound Of James Last.

THE BEST OF 150 GOLD – On 2 records/2 LP cassette
Amboss Polka, Ballad For Adeline, Charmaine, Don't Cry For Me

Argentina, Elvira Madigan: Theme, Der Einsame Hirt*, La Entrada Del Bilbao, Games That Lovers Play, Happy Heart, Happy Luxembourg, Happy music, Hora Staccato, Liechtensteiner Polka, Morgens Um Sieben Ist Die Welt Noch In Ordnung, Petersburger Schlittenfahrt, *Potpourri*: A.I.E. – Das Gibt's Nur Auf Der Reeperbahn Bei Nacht – Hier Ist Was Los – Ich Trinkt Den Wein Nicht Gernallein ; I'm On Fire – Knock On Wood – Da Kommt Jose Der Strassenmusikant – Die lustigen Holzhackerbaum – Morning Sky – Die Nacht Ist Nicht Allein Zum Schlafen Da – 1-2-3-4 . . . Fire – Pinball Wizard – Rosa Rosa, Romance No. 2 In F, Salome, Star Parade, Wenn Suss Das Mondlicht Auf Den Hügeln Schlaft.
*with Gheorghe Zamfir (Panpipes).

THE NON STOP DANCING SOUND OF THE 80's
After The Love Has Gone, Don't Stop 'Till You Get Enough, Good Times, I Was Made For Lovin' You, Knock On Wood, Lead Me On, My Sharona, Over And Over, Pop Muzik, Rise, Sad Eyes.

THE SEDUCTION
Dancing Shadows, Falling Star, Frantasy, Glow, In-Fight, It's Over, Night Drive, The Seduction: Love Theme, So Excited, Vibrations.

THIRTY-FIVE SOLID GOLD PARTY HITS
For details, see Super Party Pac.

JAMES LAST TREASURY
For details, see Non Stop Dancing 65, 66 & 66/2.

THIS IS JAMES LAST
For details, see Mr. Partyking.

TRUMPET A GOGO
American Patrol, Wheels, Granada, Never On Sunday, La Paloma, Ave Maria No Morro, Tico Tico.
Delicado, Cherry Pink And Apple Blossom White, La Bamba, Greensleeves, Mexican Hat Dance, Passion Flower, Mexico City.

TRUMPET A GOGO 2
Happy Music, Begin The Beguine, Slokiaan, La Golondrina, Donkey Serenade, Hava Nagila.
Caravan, Carmen 68, La Mer, Un Poco Rio, Always, Down By The Riverside.

TRUMPET A GOGO 3
Secret Love, Perfidia, Malagurna, Drina March, The Touch Of Your Lips, The Bandit.
Around The World, Kiss Me Honey Honey Kiss Me, Adalita, Memories Of Rubenstein, Plaisir D'Amour, Espana Cani.

TULPEN UIT AMSTERDAM
Tulpen Uit Amsterdam, Aan De Armsterdamse Grachten, Geef Mij Maar Amsterdam, Als Op Het Leidseplein De Lichtjes Weer Eens Branden Gaan, Waterloo Road, Daar Is De Orgelman.
Amsterdam, Een Pikketanussie, O Saberde Josieia, Bij Ons In De Jordaan, Omdat Ik Zoveel Van Je Hou, Onder De Bomen Van Det Plein, De Jordaan-wais, Oh Jonny, M'n Wiegie Was Een Stijfselkkisse, Ik Hou Van Jou Mooi Amsterdam, Nou Tabe Dan, Ouwe Sopraan Uit De Jordaan, Als Je Huit Ben Je Een Stakker, In De Jordon, Amsterdam (Finale).

TWENTY SOLID GOLD HITS
Aquarius, March Of The Toreadors, Happy Brasilia, Greensleeves, American Patrol, Summer Place, Bye Bye Blackbird, The Last Waltz, Mexican Hat Dance, Havah Nagilha, Games That Lovers Play, Malaguena, El Condor Pasa, Rock Around The Clock, See You Later Alligator, Hound Dog, Lara's Theme, A Man And A Woman, Happy Heart, Never On Sunday, Donkey Serenade, Hello Dolly, Milord, C'est Magnifique.

UNIQUE SOUND OF JAMES LAST
3 record set
For details, see Die Gabs Nur Einmal 2
Humba Humba A Gogo
Annchen Von Thaura.

VERY BEST OF JAMES LAST
For details, see Les Plus Grands Orchestres.

VIOLINS DANSES INTIMITE
For details, see Games That Lovers Play.

VIOLINS IN LOVE
The A That I Breathe, Was Ich Dir Sagen Will, Don't Let The Sun Go Down On Me, The Sound Of Silence, Hey Jude.

Unchained Melody, Let It Be, You Make Me Feel Brand New, A Whiter Shade Of Pale, Violins In Love.

VIOLINS IN LOVE (Japan)
As above but MacArthur Park replaces Violins In Love.

VIVA double album
First Record: Cecilia, Cuando Sali De Cuba, How Do You Do, Amazing Grace, Poppa Joe, Wedding Song, Song Sung Blue, Jesus Christ, Jenny Jenny, Killing Me Softly With His Song, Put Your Hand, Chirpy Chirpy Cheep Cheep.
Second Record: El Condor Pasa, South Of The Border, Power To The People, I Am I Said, Hot Love, The Dock Of The Bay, Ave Maria No Morro, You're So Vain, Get Ready, Jamaica Farewell, Music From Across The Way.

VOODOO PARTY
Se A Cabo, Sing A Simple Song, Heyah Masse-ga, Mamy Blue, Jin-go-lo-ba, Mr. Giant Man.
Everybody's Everything, Everyday People, U-Hambah, Inner City Blues, Babalu, Voodoo Lady Love.

VROLIJK KERSTFEEST MET
For details, see Christmas Dancing.

WEIHNACHTEN UND JAMES LAST
For details, see Christmas & James Last.

WELL KEPT SECRET
Jubilation, Summertime, I Can't Move No Mountains, Love For Sale. Bolero 75, Slaughter On Tenth Avenue, Questions, Theme From Prisoner Of Second Avenue.

WENN DIE ELISABETH
Wo Sind Deine Haare August, Was Machst Du Mit Dem Knie Lieber Hans, Warte Warte Nur Ein Weilchen, Susie, Mein Liebling Heisst Madi, Wenn Die Elisabeth, Was Kann Der Sigismund Dafur Dass Er So Schon Ist, Fraulein Pardon, Ich Hab' Das Fraul'n Helen Baden Seh'n, Sonny Boy, Schoner Gigolo, Halloh Du Susse Klingelfee, Yes We Have No Bananas, Valencia.
Veronika Der Lenz Ist Da, Blutrote Rosen, Ich Hol Dir Vom Himmel Das Blau, Santa Lucia, Du Bist Wie Die Sonne, O Madchen Mein Madchen, Vier Worte Mocht 'Ich Dir Jetzt Sagen, Wenn Die Kleinen Veilchen Bluhen, Komm In Den Park Von Sanssouci, Charleston, Black Bottom, Traumen Von Der Sudsee, Good Night Sweetheart.

WENN SUSS DAS MONDLICHT
Wenn Suss Das Mondlicht Auf Den Hugein Schlaft, (introduction), Haus Pentecost, Gaylord, Pollux, Sternlicht, Morgens Um Sieben Ist Die Welt Noch In Ordnung.
Wenn Suss Das Mondlicht (Impressionen), Ferien Am Meer, Fahrt Ans Meer, Die Welt Braucht Liebe, Becky Und Peter, Wenn Suss Das Mondlicht (Finale).

WESTERN PARTY
For details, see Country & Square Dance Party.

WITH COMPLIMENTS
For details, see James Last At His Best 1 – El Condor Pasa.

WORLD HITS
People Will Say We're In Love, September In The Rain, What Is This Thing Called Love, I Only Have Eyes For You, Charmaine. Besame Mucho, Volare, Tenderly, Singing In The Rain, I've Got You Under My Skin.

. . . Y OLE double album
Record One: Granada, La Paloma, Cherry Pink, Patricia, La Bamba, Tico Tico, Brasil, Amapola, Amor Amor Amor, Delicado, Ole O'Canganceiro, Carmen 68.
Record Two: Siboney, Malaguena, Espana Cani, Mexican Hat Dance, Valencia, Adelita, El Condor Pasa, Guantanamera, Ave Maria No Morro, Camino Verde, Perfidia.

YESTERDAY'S MEMORIES
American Patrol, I Got You Babe, Sweet Georgia Brown, Delicado, Toreadors March, Makin' Whoopee.
Greensleeves, Yesterday, La Bostella, Sail Along Silvery Moon, Adagio From Violin Concerto No. 1, Hello Dolly.

EASY LISTENING (Collection)